Praise for *The Ministry of Giving*

"I'm tired of watching churches limit their ministry impact because they lack a biblical approach to funding a bigger vision. Fortunately, this book will change your ministry to financial leaders. It offers real talk about real change in a church's capacity to fund ministry. Don't settle for being stuck. No matter what size your church, Joel, Bill, and Kimberly offer practical insights to help you take your next steps."

—**Tony Morgan**
Author, consultant, leadership coach
TonyMorganLive.com

"Want to move from a 'spray and pray' strategy of funding a ministry with letters and emails to networking and challenging your high-capacity givers? Joel, Bill, and Kimberly have assembled the practical advice a 21st century ministry needs to deepen and widen your impact for Christ. What a timely gift *The Ministry of Giving* is for the church and all Christian ministries."

—**Sam Schreiner**
Pastor, Noroton Presbyterian Church (Darien, Connecticut)

"Finally! These authors have taught me a great deal about the unique challenge of ministering to financial leaders. I'm glad their practical ideas are now in a book that will bless the Church everywhere."

—**Tim Stevens**
Executive Pastor, Granger Community Church
(Granger, Indiana)
Author of *Vision: Lost and Found* and
blogger at LeadingSmart.com

"*The Ministry of Giving* is perfectly timed in today's atmosphere of openness and awareness about generosity. The missing ingredient has been resources and relevant books on the subject for churches and church leadership. This book hits the bull's-eye and sets the standard for must-have resources for every church leader."

—Peb Jackson
Jackson Consulting Group, LLC

"Developing financial leaders is a revolutionary concept that will forever change how ministries approach stewardship. This book is the catalyst. No one understands the nature of giving like Joel, Bill, and Kimberly."

—Ben Arment
Creator of STORY and Dream Year

"In a climate of economic stress and donor fatigue, these three leaders truly understand the ministry of stewardship. They have merged donor sensitivity with a bold vision for what could be."

—Greg Ring
Co-Founder, Fulcrum Philanthropy Systems

"Working on the front lines of ministry means you don't have a lot of time for theory and philosophy. *The Ministry of Giving* is a practical guide to making things happen in a very practical and proven way. I know these authors know what they are talking about. We have raised over $12 million using their system."

—Dr. Jeff Clark
Pastor, First Hattiesburg (Hattiesburg, Mississippi)

"Every church and Christian organization has financial leaders— and God wants them to lead. Joel, Bill, and Kimberly know how to identify and nurture these leaders to the point that God's vision is fully resourced. The principles they use are not only sound, they work! I recommend this book to anyone looking to unleash their financial leaders for full Kingdom impact."

—Jamie Rasmussen
Senior Pastor, Scottsdale Bible Church (Scottsdale, AZ)

THE
MINISTRY
OF GIVING

FUND YOUR VISION BY DEVELOPING
FINANCIAL LEADERS

JOEL MIKELL, BILL MCMILLAN,
AND KIMBERLY STEWART

CONTENTS

INTRODUCTION

The ministry of giving is alive and well. And if it's not presently active in your church, it can be. Those churches experiencing abundant generosity recognize how the ministry of giving stems directly from discipleship—the process by which we become like Christ.

It is unlikely that anyone going into professional ministry ever imagined just how large a role money would play in doing ministry. There are budgets, special offerings, general giving, capital campaigns, and special-emphasis giving opportunities, just to name a few. Every one of those events can unearth lingering doubts, fears, and frustration surrounding money and ministry. Few feel prepared to handle all the rigors of ministry finances. And some feel downright betrayed that no one ever told them what to expect when it came to the challenges of fully funding Kingdom ministry.

Economic Recession Resets Giving Habits

When the Great Recession hit in 2008, a general reset took place. The healthy budget giving many churches enjoyed seemed to diminish overnight. At the same time, there was an increased demand upon churches to meet the escalating needs of community members in crisis both locally and around the world. It was an overwhelming time to be in church leadership.

The real impact of the Great Recession on church giving, felt more deeply by some than others, has been twofold. First, in most churches, these tough times diminished the economic stability of those in the middle, which affected the consistency and frequency at which they can and are willing to give. Because of that, an even greater need was placed on people who have the capacity to be financial leaders in funding local church ministry.

Unfortunately, this group is routinely disregarded by many church leaders until a financial emergency takes place. Even though the greatest dollars have often come from only a few people, financial leaders are—ironically—the most likely to be ignored by church leaders. Interaction between financial leaders and ministry leaders is nonexistent in many situations. The general lack of awareness of financial leaders in the church is holding the local church back in many ways from realizing the vision God has set before them.

A Field Guide for Ministry to Financial Leaders

Our next steps are critical for the future sustainability of local church ministry. We must act decisively, purposefully, and swiftly. But knowing what to do next is precisely the problem. There is no guidebook, no field guide written to church leaders to help them develop a ministry to those with significant financial capacity.

That is the purpose of this book. It's not about how to "fleece your flock" as some refer to the ministry of giving. Instead, we have set out to unlock the potential that exists within every church to fully fund the ministry God has placed on your heart and move forward in confidence into the chaotic conditions of postmodern local church ministry. After reading this book, you should be able to:

1. *Understand* who is—and who is not—a financial leader.

2. *Evaluate* your approach to financial leaders.

3. *Design* a plan to disciple financial leaders.

4. *Discover* and recruit financial leaders.

5. *Engage* financial leaders in Kingdom things.

6. *Ask* financial leaders for a specific amount to invest in your ministry plan.

7. *Establish* a sustainable process that can be managed and measured.

This book is not a philosophical discourse, a collection of sound bites, or a theological defense of why we should develop a ministry to financial leaders. Instead, the focus is on the design, implementation, and execution of a ministry plan that will ultimately result in a thriving giving ministry in your church.

A New Vocabulary

You've probably already noticed, but we've chosen a vocabulary that will help shape the conversation started by this book. By using these words and phrases, church leaders will begin to see the ministry of giving in a new way.

Instead of using the terms *major donors* or *high-capacity donors*, we've chosen to refer to this group as *financial leaders*. That seems to fit naturally within a ministry context. We have staff leaders, children's leaders, student leaders, adult leaders, and volunteer leaders. Why shouldn't we also have financial leaders?

Instead of *raising money*, we've chosen to refer to this process as *the ministry of giving.* There is nothing wrong with raising money, and we're not trying to hide the fact that raising money is a natural result of discipling financial leaders. Most churches have a missions ministry, an outreach ministry, and a senior adult ministry. Why shouldn't we also have a ministry of giving?

Instead of focusing our attention on *the ask*, we've chosen to place the emphasis on *discipleship*. We will certainly discuss the ask as it is part of discipling financial leaders. But the ask is a result of relational investment—not pragmatic presentation of ministry needs. Why shouldn't discipleship result in generosity and stewardship?

For too long, church leaders have attached assumptions and expectations around money and ministry that separate the two when, in fact, they are tied to each other as much as discipleship and evangelism. If you are open to reconsidering your position on the ministry of giving, we believe you will uncover an abundance of life change and ministry funding that you never have experienced before.

Practical Tools

Our hope is that this book helps jump-start the ministry of giving in your church. We designed this book to do that from the ground up. At the end of each chapter, you'll find key ideas to help you process all the material we've covered together.

In addition, we've included discussion questions at the

end of each chapter. Our hope is that you'll gather your executive leadership team and work through this book together, using the questions to process the information. This is where the best ideas will come from. And it will require the strength of everyone to put things in motion.

At the end of the book, we've put together an appendix, which includes a variety of resources we hope will help you get started immediately. You'll find scripts, job descriptions, and planning guides. We've also assembled a beginner's resource guide for tools we mention and discuss in this book.

This book is not exhaustive. It's not intended to be. Instead, we hope this begins a new conversation among your senior leadership—both paid and volunteer—around the ministry of giving.

If you will entertain and implement the ideas we have discussed in this book, we are certain you will find a group of people who will welcome your spiritual leadership and accountability. Along the way, they will exercise their gift of giving financial resources. But you'll find that they have so much more to give.

This group is highly skilled and successful because they know how to evaluate opportunities, make good decisions, plan, and regroup after an unexpected failure. Building a bridge to your financial leaders will benefit you in ways you have yet to understand or imagine.

Having helped countless church leaders walk through these steps, we can attest to the surprise so many church leaders have when we apply a fresh approach to the ministry of giving in their church. Together, we've witnessed marriages restored, addictions broken, families mended, and ministry funded beyond our wildest imaginations.

The reality is you presently have all you need to take the next step in the direction God is calling you to lead your church. But God didn't call you to go alone. The financial leaders in your church have been placed under your spiritual leadership for a reason. This is your time to activate their gifts of finances, leadership, and influence to advance the Kingdom.

We hope you are as excited about working through the material in the book as we are to share it with you. The best days of ministry are ahead of you.

Chapter One

FINANCIAL LEADERS ARE PART OF GOD'S FUNDING PLAN

God and money are not mutually exclusive. In fact, Jesus talked a lot about money. It is the single greatest external indicator of the commitments our hearts have made. While we often measure giving in dollars, the giver recognizes that money is simply an expression of the life change experienced within that informs lifestyle decisions moving forward.

Before we can appreciate the changing landscape of church giving taking place today—and how financial leaders fit into the equation of ministry funding—we need to understand a little of the history of giving within American Christianity. This will provide context for how funding ministry has adapted to the changing habits and practices within American culture.

We know with certainty that another shift is now taking place. It is reshaping how ministry is being fully funded and how it will be for the foreseeable future.

Prior to the Industrial Revolution, much of the American economy was agriculturally based, so churches received the bulk of their income at harvest time—or at least in unpredictable frequencies. So leaders of American churches were delighted by the shift to non-agrarian society because workers started to be paid weekly, making steady giving possible. And so we have the emergence of what we know today as weekly tithes and offerings.

For most of the 20th century, the American church has thrived off the regular giving of those in the middle. These are the people who give faithfully and systematically. As their incomes increased, so did the amount of their giving.

A Growing Uncertainty

Unfortunately, this certainty and confidence wouldn't last. With the fall of companies like Enron and Arthur Anderson, Americans were awakened to the reality that their secure, corporate job might not be such a sure thing after all. Then you had tragic events such as 9/11, which ushered in a series of economic and political challenges and led to the first major recession in decades.

The same church leaders who saw their budgets grow exponentially from 2000 to 2007 then saw giving plateau or decline in 2008. And so began a new era of church giving plagued by uncertainty, fear, and doubt. Churches revisited the conversation of money and ministry and recognized the rules of engagement had changed.

Church giving from the middle is no longer as stable as it once was. As more and more people are paid at varying levels and frequencies, their capacity to give regularly and increase incrementally is diminished. This new reality has opened the door for an increased dependence on financial leaders to fund ministry.

To say that undesignated giving is under fire is an understatement at best. There is undoubtedly a shift in giving taking place among the people in the pew. If there was ever a time when a broad base of congregants gave systematically, that time has passed. Giving USA reports that charitable giving has been at 2.5 percent of disposable income since 1967. Further research published in *Passing the Plate* (Oxford, 2008) documents that 20 percent of American Christians give nothing to the church. It should come as no surprise that a significant shift to financial leaders is taking place.

The modern American is more aware of the value of the dollar today than ever before. The middle wants to give, but they want to respond to more than hollow appeals and standing expectations. They want to be invited into opportunities where they can make a difference. The church may be losing ground when it comes to traditional giving techniques and practices, but people have not stopped giving or lost the desire to be involved.

The New Rules of Engagement

One-third of all charitable giving continues to be given to the religious sector, which includes churches. This amount is about $100 billion annually. That's a lot of money. So to say people have no money to give is simply uninformed. The reality is, people are giving—just not always to their church.

This new reality of giving has fostered a more empowered giver who is asking more questions, expecting to have more say in how funds are used, and demanding more results. This is the antithesis of the traditional approach to undesignated giving, which believes the giver gives to God (through the church) while the leader disburses the funds with limited accountability to the person in the pew.

The empowered giver is something to be treasured. When you can unleash the influence of a financial leader within a congregation, you will discover the energy forward momentum creates. It is no different than when you match the right person with the right volunteer role. When you match the right financial leaders with the right giving opportunities, exciting things will happen! Financial leaders are gifted to serve the church in unique ways.

Church leaders are forced to reconcile with financial leaders in a new way as the middle declines. More than 190 years after the final, predictable subsidies ended from England, American Christianity finds itself once again having to think about funding ministry in new and different ways. The modern American Christian is likely to see little difference between giving to the church and giving to a local nonprofit.

This fundamental shift in perspective moves the decision from a disciplined response informed by principles of stewardship to arbitrary generosity acted upon in the midst of an emotional experience. This puts churches in direct competition with traditional nonprofit leaders who are often more skilled at talking about money, connecting dollars to impact, and calling people to action. In the absence of the practice and belief in storehouse tithing, undesignated giving disappears.

God's Plan to Fund Ministry

We can cross our arms and deny these realities, or we can see them as an opportunity to embrace an expanded view of who will largely fund ministry moving forward. Looking to financial leaders to fill in the gap when a minor budget shortfall occurs is no longer a sound operational strategy (not that it ever was), but that approach does not honor the human relationship nor the emotion involved in any type of giving, especially giving at a significant level.

The demands of ministry are not diminishing. On the contrary, they are increasing rapidly. The good news is there is much ministry to be done, and the net result of our efforts is life change. No other institution or organization can offer that kind of return on investment. But the other side of the equation is that we must learn how to communicate with different segments of givers—and, most important, financial leaders.

Moving forward, we can no longer exclude anyone when it comes to developing a giving ministry. The work before us is too important. The lives and needs of real people are at stake.

The challenge for traditional church leaders is to borrow the time-tested lessons of the traditional nonprofit world and translate that into the language and practice of the church. The good news is that God is still interested in using His Church as a catalyst for spiritual transformation. Church leaders just need to adopt a few new approaches to match financial leaders with these giving opportunities. In addition, religious giving—as a philanthropic category—is largely stable. While some churches struggle to fund their vision, they still have home court advantage.

We must be willing to ask the hard questions, make the tough decisions, and act in courageous ways to ensure that money God intended for funding His church isn't being redirected to other organizations and causes.

Instead of seeing financial leaders as stumbling blocks, we should see them as participants in God's plan. Instead of seeing financial leaders as obstacles, we should see them as advocates and pillars of influence who can help everyone move toward God-inspired vision. Instead of seeing financial leaders as untouchable, we must recognize that they, too, need to be challenged in their spiritual journey to put into motion the gifts and resources they have been given to advance the Kingdom.

The landscape of church giving may be changing, but it is certainly not evaporating. The American church has the potential today like never before to influence more people in its community and around the world. But to bring about the Kingdom of God on earth, all God's children must be challenged and involved in stewarding what has been given to them—their time, talents, treasures, temples, and testimonies.

Giving in Response to God's Blessings

Proportionate giving provides a place and gives value to the full spectrum of giving. That spectrum begins with the "widow's mite" and extends all the way to "to whom much is given, much is required." Scripture challenges those who have been blessed with extraordinary resources to be extraordinarily generous.

Command those who are rich in this present world not to be arrogant nor to put their hope in wealth, which is so uncertain, but to put their hope in God, who

*richly provides us with everything for our enjoyment.
Command them to do good, to be rich in good deeds,
and to be generous and willing to share. In this way they
will lay up treasures for themselves as a firm foundation
for the coming age, so that they may take hold of the life
that is truly life. (1 Timothy 6:17–19)*

It is only when we release what has been abundantly given to us that God can multiply our efforts and transform our dollars into lives changed forever. No one should be left out of the conversation of money and ministry.

There are financial leaders in your church right now who are waiting for you to connect with them, inspire them, and help them see how they can be part of God's plan. They understand that God is the source of their abundance, that they are blessed for a reason—and they want to share their blessings. As pastors and church leaders, we need to speak into their lives and give them opportunities to reach their God-designed potential.

CHAPTER ONE IN REVIEW

Key Ideas

1. Giving of weekly tithes and offerings didn't become widespread until the 20th century.

2. Political and economic uncertainties began affecting churches dramatically in 2008.

3. With more Americans being paid less systematically, the church must develop new strategies for maintaining its financial stability.

4. One-third of all charitable giving continues to be given to the religious sector, which includes churches. However, many believers give to organizations and causes other than the church.

5. The challenge for church leaders is to incorporate lessons from the nonprofit world into their stewardship approaches.

Key Discussion Questions

1. What has been the giving trend in your church over the last five years?

2. What impact would it have if the top 5 percent of your givers ceased giving to the church?

3. Why do some churchgoers give to other charitable organizations and causes instead of giving to your church?

4. What are some innovative techniques you have employed in an effort to improve the financial picture in your church?

5. How can you encourage the portion of your congregation that is paid irregularly to invest in the ministries of your church?

THE MINISTRY OF GIVING IN ACTION

In early March 2011, Lead Pastor Mark Beeson publicly told the church he was specifically praying for a family to give $1 million toward the 2016 vision. Even though we've prayed for a gift of that size for years, up until that service Mark had never felt the release to say it out loud to the weekend crowd. I'm not often caught off guard by things he says, since we process nearly everything together, but this was a surprise. I thought it was very interesting that he decided to tell the congregation that we were praying for a sizable gift.

Two days after Mark told the church he was praying for a $1 million gift, I returned from a lunch meeting to messages waiting for me from a couple whom I had never met. They were five minutes away and asked if they could come right over to ask some questions about the vision and The New Normal Project (this was the project we launched to raise money for the 2016 Vision).

We had an amazing conversation, talking about life, faith, their story, and the new vision that Granger is chasing. They brought with them a copy of our brochure where we outlined the new 2016 Vision. Looking at it in this man's hands was like seeing a well-worn book. They had taken it home from the weekend series when we shared the 2016 Vision for the first time and had been living in it, reading every word over and over. They were astounded at how closely their own spiritual journey aligned with the vision that we were presenting to the congregation.

The man leaned forward and asked me with intensity, "Have you ever known that God was speaking directly to you?" He went on to tell me that this had happened to him three or four times in his life. He told me the story of a few of these times when God had given him and his wife significant direction. Each time, he explained, his hands would sweat.

The next thing this man did was ask me to leave the room.

You have to remember, we were sitting in my office. He was asking me to leave my office! Kind of funny, but he wanted to talk to his wife in private.

I stood outside my office for a few minutes, still having no idea why we were having this conversation. All I knew was this couple had been totally captured by the vision God had given the church. This was exactly what we'd been praying for as we spent months working on every word. Although I'd never met them, they seemed like the type of couple who might eventually lead a missional community.

They called me back into my office, and he continued his story: "This past weekend, when Mark said he was praying for a family to give $1 million, my hands got all sweaty, and I knew exactly what God wanted us to do."

At this point, I was thinking something spiritual...something like,..."No flippin' way!"

He continued, "We believe God wants us to commit $1 million to the church for this new vision."

I have no idea what I said next. I think I may have actually said, "No flippin' way!" I'm not sure. I'm not an emotional person, but at that moment I felt as close to tears as I ever have with total strangers. I had goose bumps on every inch of my body and was somewhat in shock.

After we finished the meeting, I sat in my office for a few minutes soaking in what had just happened . . .

The following day, I was met in the lobby with an envelope

containing a check for $1 million from people I had never even met two days earlier. We kept it very quiet for a few days while we waited for the check to clear—but then gladly announced to the church this outrageous step of faith and generosity. It was a huge boost of momentum for the church, giving us clear confirmation that we were on the right path.

It was just the first of many blessings that would come.

—Tim Stevens
Executive Pastor, Granger Community Church (Granger, IN)
Adapted from *Vision: Lost and Found*

Chapter Two

MINISTRY TO FINANCIAL LEADERS IS NOT ABOUT MONEY

There is something you need to know, but you're likely not going to believe it. Raising money is not about money. It has never been about money. It will never be about money. The people who make money the object of their fundraising efforts will never raise enough money to satisfy their needs. Never.

If raising money isn't about money, then it has to be about something else, right? You bet it is! Raising money is about uniquely and specifically directing God's provision to accomplish God's plan. This is certainly not limited to money, but it is not excluded from it either.

The ministry of giving rises and falls on our ability to build trust and permissions systems that allow church leaders to speak into the lives of the people they are ministering to. It's comfortable territory when it comes to marriage, discipleship, service, and a variety of other aspects of church ministry. But when money is introduced into the conversation, many conclude that finances and relationships are mutually exclusive.

Off Limits

Imagine the response if you went to a doctor and told him or her that you wanted a complete physical—but you wouldn't answer any questions about your heart or have any tests done on it. That's off limits. Your doctor would likely be confused. If you insisted, he or she would likely refuse to see you. It's not good medicine.

What if you went to your chiropractor and said you wanted a full adjustment—but you did not want him touching your neck? That's simply off limits. Any chiropractor worth his or her salt would again be confused and would try to explain how excluding such a critical area of the body would inhibit the good things that could happen as a result of chiropractic services.

If those examples are true, then why do so many leaders accept the premise that dealing with money—or people who have been blessed with exceptional financial resources—is off limits? We believe the reason stems from a lack of knowledge about how to engage this group within your church. We also believe this can be easily addressed with a proper strategy for discipling financial leaders.

The ministry of giving is just as legitimate as any other ministry in your church. What we do with our money is a direct reflection of what we believe about money. We are eager to preach that from the pulpit, but we stop ourselves from building relationships with certain segments of our church because we are concerned that money might corrupt our intentions or confuse the reason or purpose of the relationship.

Reasons to Opt Out

As a ministry leader, you are responsible for facilitating spiritual growth among all the people in your church—not just some of the people. That includes people who have been blessed financially. Just as ministering to parents would include a discussion about children, so too would ministering to financial leaders include a discussion about money.

Most of the leaders we talk to are simply uncertain about how to minister to financial leaders, and that uncertainty often results in avoidance. Our goal is to help you feel confident about cultivating all the resources—time, talent, and treasure—that God has already provided through the people in your church family.

Let's explore some of the top reasons why church leaders choose to opt out of ministry to financial leaders within the church:

- "I don't want to be accused of showing favoritism to people with money."

- "They would think that the only reason I am spending time with them is to ask them for money."

- "If I preach good enough and pray hard enough, God will provide."

- "People are already giving at their maximum capacity. I don't need to ask for more."

- "I don't want to spend too much time with this group, because then they will want to control the church."

- "The church shouldn't be soliciting money like schools and hospitals do."

- "We tried. It just didn't work."

This list isn't exhaustive by any means. What's unfortunate is that these preconceived ideas keep leaders from recognizing God's provision and ministering to a segment of God's people who often feel used, abused, and discarded—that is, until the financial crunch time comes. (It's no wonder that some financial leaders say their experience with church giving makes them feel like ATMs.)

Reasons to Opt In

Not every church leader has chosen to opt out of ministry to financial leaders. And—admittedly—a few have changed their minds along the way as circumstances and needs became a catalyst for relationship building among a group of people often misunderstood and pushed aside. For those church leaders who have chosen to make ministry to financial givers their responsibility, the discoveries have been profound.

Let's explore some of the feedback we've received from leaders who are actively ministering to financial leaders in their church:

- "Rich people have problems too."

- "This group wants to make a measurable difference."

- "Money is just part of the lives of financial leaders. They understand their capacity, but that doesn't make them less human—or make them superhuman."

- "Financial leaders ask a different set of questions than the average church giver asks."

- "Lead givers are results-oriented but are comfortable with failure—as long as learning happens in the process."

- "Church-wide vision motivates financial leaders to participate in ways God has uniquely gifted them."

- "Financial leaders think about giving as an investment opportunity, not a tax-avoidance strategy."

- "Financial leaders want to be part of doing ministry, but it is unlikely they will ever fill the traditional volunteer roles."

The primary reason more church leaders aren't ministering to financial leaders is, in large part, due to a failure to communicate. At the end of the day, the church leader must reach out and create those bridge-building opportunities to make a human connection. The future vitality and sustainability of local church ministry depend on it.

A Full Plate

Have you ever been somewhere for a special dinner and couldn't fit all the food you wanted onto one plate? Maybe it was Thanksgiving at Mom's or Christmas at Grandma's. Whatever the occasion, you had to find another plate or come back for a second round after you finished round one. There was no way you were going to fit all the food you wanted onto the single plate you had in hand.

The same is true in your ministry. You likely have a full plate. And it's unlikely that ministry to financial leaders was ever written into your job description! (We hope by the end of this book it will be, though.)

That means you have an important decision to make. If you decide ministry to financial leaders is something God is calling you to do, then what are you willing to get off your plate so you can make room for ministering to this specific group? Making such changes isn't easy, but doing so doesn't mean anyone else is less important. We have staff members for different segments of our congregation because we want someone to be dedicated to the needs of each group. The same approach is needed for ministry to financial leaders.

Raise People, Not Money

If you are the senior leader or part of your church's executive leadership team, then this responsibility falls to you. We'll unpack more about what that looks like and what new staff positions this effort might create later. But ministry to financial leaders—just like every other initiative—doesn't work unless it is coming directly from the top.

All God's children need guidance from some spiritual leader. This is exactly what Jesus meant when He described Himself as the Good Shepherd. Within the context of local church ministry, that means we must minister to every part of our congregation. We can't ignore one group out of the false assumption that financial leaders don't need their pastor as much as other people do.

God has provided you with everything your congregation

needs to take the next step in advancing Kingdom ministry. Perhaps the fullness of His provision resides within a group that has not been spiritually challenged to participate in the ways God has uniquely and specifically gifted them. God is not preoccupied with money, so we shouldn't be either. However, He is preoccupied with all His children—even those to whom He has given great financial resources.

Raising money begins when we become exclusively focused on raising people to accomplish God's plan and vision.

CHAPTER TWO IN REVIEW

Key Ideas

1. People who make money the main objective of their fundraising efforts will never raise enough money.

2. How people handle money is a spiritual growth issue.

3. There are financial leaders within your congregation who are willing and able to invest in causes that advance God's Kingdom.

4. God has provided you with everything your congregation needs to take the next step toward bringing God-inspired vision to reality.

5. Raising money begins when we focus on raising people to accomplish the purpose and vision of the church.

Key Discussion Questions

1. Who are the financial leaders within your congregation?

2. On a scale of 1 to 10, with 10 being totally comfortable, how comfortable are you approaching financial leaders about engaging in the ministry and vision of the church?

3. If the financial stability of the church is dependent upon the strength of your discipleship ministry, what is the financial growth potential within your church?

4. List the resources you have available to help you minister to financial leaders within your church.

5. What do you need to move off of your plate so you can focus on ministry to financial leaders?

Chapter Three

QUESTIONS CHURCH LEADERS HAVE ABOUT FINANCIAL LEADERS

Ministry and money are clearly intertwined. Just like Bible reading, prayer, and service are parts of the Christian experience, so is giving. To try to keep them separate only inhibits your ability to realize the dreams and vision God has given you.

Further, failing to challenge every person in your congregation to grow in every spiritual discipline robs them of the blessing God intended to give them through the practice and discipline of faith. We aren't doing anyone a service by avoiding the subject of giving. Instead, we are limiting their ability to make an impact in the Kingdom.

If so much is at stake, who is primarily responsible for the funding of ministry? Is it the church leader or the financial leader? One could argue it is both—and that would be true. But the church leader is called to facilitate spiritual growth through discipleship. Since giving is a spiritual issue first and a financial concern second, it falls under the realm of the church leader to challenge every member of the congregation to grow in the practice of giving along with other spiritual gifts.

Practice and Resources Needed

Most leaders recognize that funding ministry has changed dramatically. A smaller (but growing) group of leaders would affirm that raising money is more about raising people than dollars and cents. Still, when it comes to connecting with financial leaders, why do so many church leaders continue to avoid the call to minister to them—or worse run away from them?

We certainly don't think it is the result of a lack of knowledge or commitment to ministry. Most church leaders are highly educated and very intentional individuals. They are passionate about seeing God change lives and feel divinely called to the roles they fill.

Quite often senior leaders recognize the need to engage financial leaders but are burdened by two things—fear and doubt. This fear and doubt stem from a lack of experience in, and a lack of resources for, ministering to financial leaders. When church leaders have the resources they need to engage financial leaders, there is no limit to what can happen in the lives of people through the ministry of giving.

Questions That Cause Anxiety

A major component of this avoidance is church leaders' concerns that they don't have anything to offer financial leaders. Again, our experience tells us that the financial leader is much more concerned about disappointing the church leader than the other way around. We'll explore more about the mind of the financial leader in chapter 4.

Let's unpack some of the common questions that cause

many church leaders to experience anxiety at the thought of connecting with financial leaders:

1. *What if I offend financial leaders by reaching out to them?* It is nearly impossible to do this unless you are rude, crass, or generally unpleasant. It is unlikely you are in ministry if this is your personality. There is no offense in connecting with members of your congregation to build relationships. Your primary goal is to get to know people, learn what they are passionate about, and discover what questions they wrestle with.

2. *I've never been around people with money. What if I say or do the wrong thing?* People with money are just like everyone else. They have the same struggles in marriage, pressures at work, and troubles with their teenagers that every spouse, professional, and parent does. Money does not solve problems. In some instances, it complicates them.

3. *What if they tell me no?* If they tell you they can't meet, it's likely a scheduling conflict. Financial leaders usually carry great professional responsibility. Don't be offended if you have to wait a week or two to get some time with them. It's unlikely that every financial leader will decline an invite, so continue to extend invitations and work with the people who are able to meet. Remember, at this point the intention is just to connect with financial leaders in your church, not to specifically ask for money. We'll talk about asking for money in chapter 9.

4. *What if they don't have confidence in me?* Remember that financial leaders are likely to be intimidated by you. They know the business world, but they see you as the spiritual leader—an area of their lives they are less certain about. It's likely they will be looking to you for wisdom.

5. *What if they ask a question that I can't answer?* No one expects you to have all the answers. It's okay to say, "I don't know. I'll have to get back to you on that." Expect financial leaders to ask lots of questions. They are used to being in a position of processing lots of details and data, drawing conclusions, and then deciding significant next steps. This is part of how God built them and why they are successful.

6. *Will they use our time together to criticize me or a decision the church has made?* If they are willing to talk to you about a hurtful experience, see that as an opportunity to connect with them and right any wrongs. Financial leaders don't typically hesitate to share their thoughts. If they want to express something, they will. If they express their thoughts to you, it is a sign of trust and respect.

7. *What will other leaders and members think if they know I am meeting with particular individuals or couples?* Your role is to minister to your congregation. Spending time with people is how you build relationships and earn the permission to speak into their lives. If you are a senior leader, then you are uniquely positioned to connect with the

financial leaders in your church. They see you as a peer and equal. Top leaders want to engage with other top leaders.

These are the questions we hear most often from church leaders as reasons why they hesitate to connect with financial leaders in their church. The most important thing we want you to know is that it's normal to feel uncertain around people, situations, and circumstances that are not familiar to us. We want to challenge you to face your uncertainties and then move forward to be the spiritual leader your financial leaders need.

Left Alone

Let's consider what happens when financial leaders are left to figure out their own spiritual growth:

- They may never be fully connected to your church.

- They may never fully exercise the gifts God has given them—including, but not limited to, giving.

- They may never grow spiritually to understand their place and important role within the Kingdom.

- They may never realize their church needs them— even when there is not a crisis.

- They may never find in their job, accomplishments, or financial statement the kind of peace, satisfaction, and hope that come from ministry partnership.

- They may never influence other financial leaders to grow in their giving.

- They may never consider the church as a viable, alternative channel for the abundance they will pass on to other organizations and causes.

If financial leaders are left alone, they will never know their pastor loved, cared for, and respected them. The very successful often have few people who can be trusted to act with pure intentions. The church leader is uniquely gifted to play the role of the spiritual leader in the life of a financial leader. Don't let the lack of practice and resources prevent you from ministering to the most neglected segment of the congregation.

Begin the Journey—Together

Church leaders don't shy away from reaching out to any other group of people in the church, so why should they avoid financial leaders? There is room for everyone in the Kingdom of God. You have the honor of ministering to this small demographic that has unique needs, cultivating their spiritual maturity so they become financial leaders in the church.

The great paradox is that you, too, will grow as you lead financial leaders in your church to grow in grace and truth. Together, your journey will take you places you never anticipated. Financial leaders will claim victories they never thought possible. And your church will reach heights of ministry no one previously thought attainable.

Your journey begins with the willingness to push through the fear and doubt and say yes to the people God has given to you to grow, minister to, and cultivate for Kingdom impact. This is your moment to step out in faith and trust that God will bless your obedience and faithfulness to lead His church to accomplish the vision He has entrusted to you.

CHAPTER THREE IN REVIEW

Key Ideas

1. When we avoid the topic of giving, we do the people in our church more harm than good.

2. There are people called and equipped to invest in the financial ministry of your church.

3. Church leaders must make every effort to build trusting relationships with financial leaders in their congregations.

4. If financial leaders are left to figure out spiritual growth on their own, they will fall short of their potential.

5. As you lead the financial leaders within your church, you will grow in your awareness of the valuable role they play in the ministry of the church.

Key Discussion Questions

1. When was the last time you led the church through a series on money? What was the outcome?

2. How can you become more aware of the financial leaders within your congregation?

3. What are three things you can do to develop a trusting relationship with financial leaders in your church?

4. What is your strategy for guiding the spiritual development of financial leaders?

5. What are some keys roles that financial leaders in your church can fill?

The Ministry of Giving in Action

Brad and Emily's story of financial leadership is truly inspiring. They are business owners who began tithing even when the business was struggling. They are committed to generosity and giving to their church. Brad and Emily like knowing the ministry vision and the challenges as it's important to them in order to pray about their financial role and support. They say that staying connected to their senior pastor and vision are meaningful. These meetings have resulted in steady increases in giving—39 percent one year, 64 percent after the next. The ownership these leaders have in their church's vision is astounding.

—Eagle Brook Church (Centerville, MN)

Chapter Four

UNDERSTAND THE MIND
OF THE FINANCIAL LEADER

I (Joel) remember my early days in ministry, serving on the staff of a church that was full of high net worth individuals. One night I was out with a church member who had become a friend—and also happened to be a multimillionaire.

I did not grow up in the lap of luxury. We never wanted for anything, but I was not born with a silver spoon in my mouth. This friend and I were driving in the car and carrying on a conversation about something insignificant when I decided to ask him exactly what I had thought about asking him a million times before.

I looked over at him and asked, "What does it feel like to be a millionaire?" He smiled and responded, "Joel, I'm no smarter than you. I'm no better than you. I'm just richer than you. For whatever reason, I was in the right place at the right time to make an investment in a new business startup, and God blessed the business beyond my wildest dreams. I don't know why God chose me. But I'll tell you this— I am incredibly thankful for the blessings entrusted to me and grateful I can give generously. My greatest desire now is to make a difference in the lives of people. Because I'm blessed, I'm thankful."

Today, when I meet with pastors who have uncertainty about ministering to financial leaders, I share that conversation with them. There is always a smile—and sometimes a laugh—but everyone understands what I'm saying.

Financial leaders aren't big, scary monsters looking to destroy church leaders and foil their ministry plans. That is pure fiction. Financial leaders are looking to be part of something they are passionate about and leverage their gifts and resources to accomplish Kingdom things. For all the anxiety around the ministry of giving, everyone involved wants to achieve the same thing—life change.

Common Observations

Now that we've unpacked in chapter 3 how church leaders often feel toward financial leaders, we want to consider how financial leaders view the church, giving, and their pursuit of significance. We think you'll be surprised by what you're about to read. Of course, we don't claim to be experts on the minds of financial leaders, but we've spent enough time with them to feel comfortable listing some common characteristics shared among a vast majority of the financial leaders we've worked with. Based on some common observations about how financial leaders see the world, we can surmise that:

- Financial leaders want a relationship with senior leaders of the organizations they support—including their church.

- Financial leaders see giving as a privilege, not an obligation. They have been blessed and want to give back, but they will not give—significantly—out of any sense of duty.

- Financial leaders understand the need for things like technology, buildings, and staff. They understand the costs and benefits of assembling the right set of tools to accomplish the task at hand.

- Financial leaders desire to be part of something bigger than themselves and to play a role in solving a specific problem they are passionate about.

- Financial leaders are never offended when someone asks them for money. The greatest offense would be not asking at all.

- Financial leaders want to use their financial resources to establish a legacy.

- Financial leaders covet a personal relationship with their pastor. As key leaders, who else could they trust enough to seek advice, ask for help, or just voice frustrations?

- Financial leaders want their pastor and church leaders to see them as ordinary—not superhuman.

- Financial leaders believe they have a lot more to offer than just money. They've been at the decision-making table at critical junctures and would love to be able to contribute to the success of their church in that way.

- Financial leaders understand that you don't talk to everyone the same way. Speak to financial leaders about specifics, results, expectations, and plans. This is their language.

- Financial leaders accept that failure is part of the equation of success. As long as there is an effort by church leaders to understand the cause behind failures, financial leaders can be confident progress is being made.

- Financial leaders recognize what they have is the result of their effort and God's blessing. As a result, they want to give back in a meaningful way.

- Financial leaders know that it is hard for church leaders to talk about money with them. They want to help church leaders get over that and be successful. Financial leaders are on your side.

- Financial leaders appreciate it when other people speak to them plainly and directly. They are straightforward and direct in their communication preferences and habits.

- Financial leaders expect results. This is what the business world admires and rewards. They've achieved much and understand how success creates momentum and opportunity.

- Financial leaders desire to help their church be as successful at reaching people as possible. It's not about control but about offering strategic insight in the moment of need.

- Financial leaders are regularly asked for donations from lots of organizations but rarely—if ever—the church. Sadly, many never consider giving to the church in a significant way because they have never been asked to do so.

- Financial leaders need to have confidence that the plan of action is clearly articulated, church leadership can be trusted, and the follow-through is consistent. Trust is a big deal with financial leaders. That's why relationships are key to the ministry of giving.

- Financial leaders never see church giving as part of tax planning but always see it as part of an investment plan. Some church leaders believe financial leaders are motivated by tax deductions. Large gifts are rarely prompted by tax deadlines. Instead, they are driven by need and opportunity.

If you've never spent much time with financial leaders to know these things firsthand, we hope this list gives you insight into the financial leader mindset. We also hope you're encouraged to see that you likely have a lot in common and much to talk about. Financial leaders are human too. The difference is they have significant experience and bring a great deal of success to the table. Because of their success, they want to make sure they make the most of the resources they have to give.

Rules of Engagement

When you talk to financial leaders, you will want to do your homework in advance. Their most valued asset is time, and it's the one thing they have very little of. This is why you should be encouraged when they give you time to meet.

There are a lot of people and things pulling at them and calling for their attention. Their calendars are booked solid. When they give you time to meet, you'll need to be ready to go. As you prepare for your conversations with financial leaders, here are some general rules of engagement:

- *Know that financial leaders are already giving to a variety of other organizations.* If you want them to get further involved in your church, you need to be prepared to show them where they're needed and how they can make a unique contribution to accomplish something that is personal to them.

- *Financial leaders want to understand the why, how, and what of any strategy decision a church leader makes.* We're talking about vision and mission decisions. Remember, they are used to sitting at the decision-making table. They don't want to take over your job; they already have enough responsibility. But they do want assurance that you have all your bases covered.

- *You need to be ready to share specific details if they ask.* That doesn't mean having all the answers, but it does mean demonstrating you've thought your ideas through.

- *Respect your time with them.* Have a purpose in meeting with them. Follow up and follow through on everything they ask. Show them that you value them and their time.

- *Please don't forget to be human.* Ask them about their life, their spouse, their children, and what they like to do when they aren't a busy professional. Few people ask them these types of questions. It also helps ease into a relationship built on mutual trust and respect.

Different Is Always a Little Awkward at First

Joel's experience described at the beginning of this chapter is an important one. Financial leaders are just like everyone else. They are passionate people who want to find a community of people that share their beliefs and passions. They want to make a difference, and they absolutely see their success as leverage to accomplish big things.

We can't lose sight of whom we are talking to. We wouldn't talk to a sixteen-year-old the same way we would talk to a six-year-old, would we? Of course not! The same is true for financial leaders. Talk to them and interact with them in ways that are consistent with their personality, education, and experience. The more time you spend with financial leaders, the more comfortable you'll become being around them.

It's going to feel awkward at first. You may even stumble and stutter through a few meetings and interactions. That's okay. Make sure you are genuine and do your best to make the most of every interaction.

If you'll do that, you'll discover what so many other church leaders have already: Financial leaders know they have the ability to significantly impact the trajectory of the organizations and causes they are passionate about. They are receptive to church leaders who recognize what they can offer—in time, resources, and insight.

CHAPTER FOUR IN REVIEW

Key Ideas

1. Financial leaders are looking to be part of something they are passionate about and leverage their gifts and resources to accomplish Kingdom things.

2. Financial leaders are never offended when someone asks them for money. The greatest offense would be not asking at all.

3. Financial leaders are invested in many organizations. As a church leader, be prepared to present your organization as worthy of consideration because of its mission and purpose.

4. Financial leaders are passionate people who want to find a community of people that share their beliefs and passions. They want to invest in things that matter.

5. The more time you spend around financial leaders, the more comfortable you will be talking to them about your vision and how they can support it.

Key Discussion Questions

1. Based on what you know about the financial leaders in your church, what are some issues that stir their passion?

2. What church strategies parallel the interests of financial leaders?

3. Why should financial leaders consider supporting the ministries of your church?

4. How is your church making a difference in your community? What is the best way to communicate this information with financial leaders?

5. Who are two or three financial leaders you believe you could easily talk to?

Chapter Five

WHAT FINANCIAL LEADERS WISH THEY COULD SAY TO THEIR PASTOR

Financial leaders are comfortable meeting with other leaders in their context. Whether it's a business meeting, seminar, or political discussion, the financial leader is prepared. He or she has been there before. Environments that might make most people nervous or unsure of themselves are normal for these individuals.

But when it's time to meet with a pastor, financial leaders can be downright unsure of what to expect. Many wonder if they will end up disappointing the person they consider a spiritual leader. When church leaders and financial leaders meet, the anxiety is mutual.

We've already considered what church leaders can do to prepare to meet with financial leaders. Preparation and practice certainly help ease any anxiety. Another way to ease the discomfort is to remember some relational basics. Simple conversation is the basis of every relationship. Our level of disclosure is directly proportional to the level of comfort between two individuals. The more conversation you have with someone, the more natural the flow of interaction will become. As with all relationships, church leaders and financial leaders need to develop comfort over time. As comfort increases, so will the level of sharing.

As you begin to reach out to the financial leaders within your church, we want you to consider some of the things that financial leaders—especially those who don't have an ongoing dialogue with their pastor—wish they could say to their pastor.

Failure to Communicate

Communication flows freely in the midst of a relationship. The same is true with financial leaders. The more time you spend with them, the more comfortable they will become engaging you with the thoughts that are running through their minds.

Some church leaders might argue that if financial leaders want to say something, they should come out and say it. While that might be true, we don't treat any other segment of our congregations like that, do we? Of course not!

The first step of any relationship requires communication. A lack of communication will never foster community. If we have an ongoing relationship with someone, we can tell when something is off and when things are going well. When we are walking alongside financial leaders and doing life together, it will create the trust and respect necessary for open conversations about personal things, spiritual things, and other important issues the financial leader might be wrestling with.

Unspoken Requests

As you spend more time with financial leaders in your church, you'll discover a rich history of experience and perspective. You'll discover they hold a lot of respect for you. And if you are able to build a bridge of trust, you'll uncover some unspoken requests.

It's worth noting that financial leaders aren't always warm and fuzzy, and this crowd isn't known for its eagerness to share feelings in a support group or similar environment. They might not use these words, but we are confident the statements listed below are absolutely things financial leaders wants to say to their church leaders.

- *"Don't be afraid of me."* Financial leaders are left alone by many church leaders for reasons we have explored. While financial leaders might present well in public, everyone wants to be liked, valued, and appreciated. No one wants to be feared by others to the point they are avoided.

- *"I'm normal."* Financial leaders want you to see them as normal. Don't get lost in the size of their houses, the types of cars they drive, or the extravagance of their vacations. (Of course, some financial leaders are very unsuspecting people who don't live extraordinary lifestyles at all.) They are humans who struggle just like everyone else.

- *"I need to be able to trust you."* Financial leaders are surrounded by people who want to use them because of who they are and what they have. Most of these leaders feel very alone, even though they are very much in the middle of a crowd. They never know whom to trust—but they want to trust their pastor.

- *"Please don't judge me."* Money doesn't always fix problems. It can often hide them. If financial leaders let you into their lives, they don't want to be judged. They likely need help. They need a spiritual leader to speak into their lives.

- *"I hope I say the right things."* Financial leaders don't like disappointing people they hold in high esteem. They don't want to say or do anything that might make you think less of them. How other people perceive them is important to them, because they believe how you perceive them determines the type of interactions they will have with you.

Landing in the Comfort Zone

While financial leaders might feel less confident about their ability to walk through the land mines of theology and church ministry, they are very comfortable when it comes to business or financial conversations. This is their sweet spot. The sooner you can get them talking about the things they know, are interested in, and are most comfortable talking about, the more enjoyable the conversation will be for both of you.

Almost all financial leaders have a similar set of questions they ask themselves, their business partners, and people and organizations they choose to invest in. If you can become familiar with these questions and be prepared to speak to them, then you'll feel more prepared and the financial leaders will affirm that you are the leader they want to support.

Please know that these questions are not interview style questions. They will come in the midst of conversation in a variety of wording styles and structures. But be aware that your answers to these questions will be an important way financial leaders evaluate just how much they want to invest in you. (Never forget that people give to people. This is why relationships and trust are so important.)

The following are some top-of-mind questions that financial leaders have:

- *"What's your vision?"* They want to know more than what's possible. They need to have confidence that you know how to get there.

- *"Why this vision?"* Your ability to answer this is important. You won't be able to hide your intentions here. You have to be honest and articulate. *Why* comes before *what* and *how* every time.

- *"What difference will achieving this vision make?"* Results are always key. Financial leaders completely buy into Stephen Covey's principle that we should always "begin with the end in mind." Their perception of the potential impact will directly influence their level of support.

- *"Why now?"* Just because your vision sounds good doesn't mean the timing is right. Success is just as much about timing as it is about planning. Be prepared to discuss the immediacy and urgency of achieving your vision specifically. Church leaders are comfortable speaking in ambiguous terms. Financial leaders are not. They are typically very analytical people who think in concrete terms and constructs.

A Long Way to the Ask

If you've been avoiding financial leaders because you are afraid of asking them for money, we hope you're beginning to see that the ask comes much, much later in the conversation. You have a lot of ground to cover before you get there. The better prepared you are at connecting with financial leaders on a relational level and the better prepared you are to address their most-pertinent questions, the easier it will be to ask for some type of commitment when the opportunity presents itself.

Anticipating what financial leaders wish they could say to their pastor will force church leaders to not only do their homework but become more specific, detailed, and results-focused. This can only be a good thing. Your preparation will sharpen your thoughts and help you become an even more compelling speaker to your entire congregation.

What so many church leaders discover is that both parties have a lot to learn from each other. It is not a one-way street. Instead, it is a complementary relationship that results in even greater ministry capacity. We like to think God intended it to be like that all along.

CHAPTER FIVE IN REVIEW

Key Ideas

1. The more time financial leaders spend with you, the more comfortable they will be sharing their thoughts with you.

2. If you wait for the congregation to make the first move, many ministries will be paralyzed.

3. Most financial leaders have great respect for their pastors and church leaders.

4. Financial leaders expect you to be able to explain your vision, why it is important, what will happen if you don't go for it, and why pursuing the vision is important now.

5. The better prepared you are at connecting with financial leaders on a relational level and the better prepared you are to address their most-pertinent questions, the easier it will be to ask for some type of commitment when the opportunity presents itself.

Key Discussion Questions

1. Think about your weekly schedule. When is the best time for you to meet with financial leaders? What do you think is the best time for them to meet?

2. Why is it important for church leaders to drive ministries rather than waiting for the congregation to initiate them?

3. Who are some of the unsuspecting financial leaders in your church? These are the people who have considerable financial resources but are behind the scenes.

4. Prepare an elevator talk (no more than two minutes) that explains your vision and its urgency.

5. List three key financial leaders in your church. What, other than their financial status, do you know about each of them? What would you like to know?

THE MINISTRY OF GIVING IN ACTION

I have learned that financial leaders *want* and even *long* to be part of what God is doing at their church. Like any other believers with spiritual gifts, they long to exercise theirs for God's Kingdom glory. It's the pastor's responsibility to help financial leaders step into the opportunities that allow them to use their gifts. The pastor's role is spiritual, not financial—we simply paint the vision picture, call into the journey, ask for a commitment, and celebrate God's result. I have learned to never underestimate God's ability to call deep into the heart of a financial leader.

—Dr. Tom Pfizenmaier
Senior Minister, Bonhomme Presbyterian Church
(Chesterfield, MO)

Chapter Six

CHALLENGES TO ESTABLISHING A GIVING MINISTRY

If you've read this far in the book, there is something we've discussed that is resonating with you. We spent the first half of the book talking about the *why* and the *what* surrounding the ministry of giving. Now we want to turn our attention to the *how*. We believe the next five chapters will give you all you need to get started developing a ministry of giving in your church.

Any time you launch something new, there will be challenges. Challenges aren't bad, and you shouldn't be discouraged by them. The best thing you can do is anticipate them and know what you will do next. There will be surprises along the way, but what you will gain through building intentional relationships with financial leaders in your church will far outweigh any and all obstacles you must overcome.

The roadblocks we outline aren't unusual or out of the ordinary for anyone who launches a ministry of giving. You are in good company. And you should know that those who have gone before you have been successful at overcoming every single one of them.

All Alone

If everything we have stated up to this point is true, then why isn't everyone pursuing a ministry of giving in their church? That's a fair question. We think there are some specific reasons why everyone hasn't jumped on board yet:

- *This is still a very new conversation within church ministry.* As it matures and more churches adopt this ministry endeavor, you'll see and hear more about it.

- *Some of the first churches to attempt a ministry of giving didn't get it right the first time.* This has fueled a general resistance for many church leaders—for now, at least.

- *Some leaders don't know what they don't know.* It's like trying to tell your toddler not to jump off the couch. Sometimes they just have to figure it out for themselves.

- *There is a general lack of expectation that the church should be developing a giving ministry.* This, of course, is not true for other areas of church ministry.

- *There aren't a lot of good, successful examples of churches doing this.* Success begets success. When more churches establish a giving ministry, the more normal it will be for others to intentionally invest in this segment of the congregation.

We want to be clear that none of these reasons is an indictment against church leaders or the church itself. We would never condemn anyone for coming to a different conclusion. We believe, however, that an open mind to the ministry of giving will unleash a funding capacity that will fuel Kingdom growth and expansion in ways never previously thought possible.

None of the above reasons means you can't be successful launching a ministry of giving. But you'll need to be prepared so you know what to expect. This will influence your planning, communication, and execution.

Different Expectations

Both nonprofits and churches depend on supporters or members to generously provide participation, service, and dollars to accomplish a social, economic, or political mission. In spite of the similarities that exist, however, there are some distinct differences.

- Few church leaders see fundraising as an essential part of their role. Nonprofits understand that without funding they can't operate.

- Few churches have a dedicated staff member focused on financial development. Nonprofits understand that a development director is an essential staff role that boosts the lifeblood of the organization.

- Few church leaders are comfortable talking about the need for money. Nonprofits understand that funding is their number one priority.

- Only a few churches have dedicated specific efforts toward a ministry of giving. Nonprofits are always looking for ways to multiply their giving base by dedicating time and effort to the cause.

- Few church leaders are ready to defend staff positions or program efforts that appear to be all about money. Nonprofits make no apologies about money being part of their planning and decision making.

We certainly don't expect churches to act like nonprofits. That's not what we are suggesting. But we do believe it's time to change our approach to developing financial leaders in the local church.

So many times church leaders want to compare themselves to other churches and leaders and wait for an approach to become mainstream before adopting it for their own church. Moving forward with this approach as an early adopter, however, will be well worth the effort. Developing your financial leaders is in line with biblical teaching, something that will further Kingdom work. Even if you are one of the few heading down this path in your community, the sooner you implement the approach, the sooner you will see growth and maturity in your church community.

Assembling the Ministry of Giving Team

As you prepare to launch a ministry of giving, you'll need a minimum of three types of people: the senior pastor, a volunteer or dedicated staff member, and a couple of financial leaders who are willing to be early adopters. If you don't have all three, we recommend waiting until you do to move forward.

1. *The senior pastor.* They are key to their teams, setting the tone and expectations for other staff and volunteer members. They should know that

financial leaders will want to interact with and have access to the senior pastor to develop the ministry.

2. *A volunteer or dedicated staff member.* These people will facilitate all the meetings—from setup to follow-up. They will also coordinate all meeting details, any special events, and more. We do not recommend appointing the senior pastor's administrative assistant to this role because it requires at least one person's full attention. Of course, those chosen for this role at their churches should be consistent in giving, but they don't necessarily need to be financial leaders. They need to have a comfort level of interacting with people in executive roles. Otherwise, they'll be too intimidated to make the necessary connections within their congregations. For an expanded description of this critical role, see "Sample Job Description for Executive Director" in the appendix.

3. *Early Adopters.* You'll want to have one to three financial leaders on board with you. It will help you avoid some pitfalls, affirm your leadership, and help you navigate new territory with other financial leaders. It's always best to let a peer influence another peer. These financial leaders will help you outline a plan of action and will also follow through to make sure it's a success. The early adopters will think of things many church leaders would never consider and will bring a fresh perspective to the mix.

We can't emphasize enough that you shouldn't go down this road as a lone ranger. Not only will it feel impossible, your failure rate will be high. If you make too many mistakes, you could damage your credibility in this effort and perhaps other parts of your ministry. You also shouldn't go down this road alone, because you don't have to.

Roadblocks Are Opportunities to Grow

Roadblocks aren't reasons not to do something significant. Every financial leader in your church understands what it's like to stand up against the odds and accomplish something that other people thought was impossible. They will respect you for blazing new territory.

Even more important is that you are talking about engaging a group within your church that can make a significant impact on your ministry both now and in the future. Financial leaders are powerful igniters of ministry. Don't underestimate the role God designed them to play within the church.

Roadblocks are opportunities to grow. Your faith will be stretched. Your skill set will be expanded. You will place yourself in a position to learn and expand as a leader. Those are moments when God can shape you into the leader you were destined to be so you are prepared to advance the Kingdom through local church ministry. Embrace the roadblocks; don't allow them to be a reason not to move forward in launching a ministry of giving.

CHAPTER SIX IN REVIEW

Key Ideas

1. Roadblocks aren't bad; they are a predictable part of launching anything new.

2. An open mind to the ministry of giving will unleash a funding capacity for ministry that will fuel Kingdom growth and expansion in ways never previously thought possible.

3. The tension between money and ministry must be mitigated as the church works toward a new era of giving.

4. Success in the ministry of giving requires three key leaders prior to initiation: the senior pastor must be on board, a volunteer or staff member must be dedicated to the ministry, and early adopters must set the example.

5. Every financial leader in your church understands what it's like to stand up against the odds and accomplish something that other people thought was impossible. They will respect you for blazing new territory.

Key Discussion Questions

1. What are some of the potential challenges you might face as you move toward the ministry of giving?

2. What are some of the potential giving-related wins associated with doing something you've never done before?

3. In what ways has the lack of financial resources affected the ministry potential of your church?

4. Do you have each of the following? (1) senior pastoral leadership and support in the giving ministry; (2) a volunteer or staff member dedicated to overseeing the ministry; (3) one to three early adopters who are willing to publicly support the ministry.

5. Fast forward to being on the other side of your vision. What difference will your church make in the community? How will God's Kingdom be advanced?

Chapter Seven

HOW TO IDENTIFY
FINANCIAL LEADERS

With the right team in place, you are ready to launch a ministry of giving in your church. All you need to do now is be sure you can identify those financial leaders. This isn't a one-time event. You'll need to create a system you can monitor and measure, so you'll know if you're being effective or not.

Identifying financial leaders doesn't have to be as awkward as an eighth-grade dance, but it might feel that way if you're not sure how to start. You can't just start asking people after Sunday services how much they are worth. There are some obvious places to look and ways to approach this discovery process.

Let's start with the most obvious place—your church contribution list. If you have a policy in place that the senior pastor doesn't look at giving details, then identify another executive staff member to do this. Another alternative is to have your business administrator or whoever manages your contributions create a list of names who give significantly each year (you may want to hide the actual dollar amounts, however).

And that brings up a crucial point: You can't launch a giving ministry if no one is monitoring *what* people give.

Going with your "gut" on this one is a really, really bad idea. Sometimes the people you think are financial leaders actually are, but you are sure to discover several financial leaders you had never suspected.

Contribution History

As the list is developed from the contribution list, you'll want to look for these things:

- *Total annual giving.* Financial leaders rarely give with regular frequency because they aren't necessarily paid as everyone else is. Many of them earn a good deal of their income from investments, bonuses, or commissions. Looking at the total number with all funds combined will help you discern if this person is a financial leader or not. As a general rule of thumb, start looking for annual amounts equal to or greater than $10,000 to $12,000. Because some financial leaders are not giving at their maximum capacity, this is a good range to consider.

- *Frequency of giving.* If the gifts are coming in similar amounts and follow a consistent pattern, then the giver is likely giving out of earned income, not liquid assets. If you see an irregular pattern with unusually high points three to four times a year, then you're more in line with how a financial leader is likely to give.

- *Length of giving.* Another place to find financial leaders is by looking at special offerings or initiatives. If someone donates $20,000 to international missions during a one-time special offering, this giver would fit the giving habits of a financial leader.

- *Method of giving.* Many large gifts are made electronically via stock transfer, bank checks, and even using credit cards. This is really a convenience feature that makes it simple for a large gift to be completed and the money to be transferred. You should also consider large gifts coming from investment funds, charitable trusts, or donor advised funds too.

- *First-time gifts.* When a large gift is made from someone the church has no record for, then you may have discovered a financial leader. While all first-time givers should be considered, any gift of $5,000 or more should automatically fall within this category.

- *Special gifts.* Individuals' previous gift totals from past capital fund campaigns or special initiatives might also reveal some financial leaders in your church. This category should also include year-end gifts. These are event-driven or time-sensitive giving opportunities. If a large gift is made during these times, it is consistent with the giving habits of a financial leader.

Executive Team and Ministry Directors

Once you have a working list of names, you'll want to discuss the names among a small group of executive level and ministry directors. This should be done with discretion as you don't want that list distributed via social media, email, or—worse—in print. Contextualizing the process and setting appropriate privacy expectations should be enough to settle any concerns or questions.

You want to discover who has a relationship with whom. As you seek to reach out to the financial leaders in your church, it is best to do so within the context of an existing relationship. If a relationship already exists, then ask for an introduction or a connection to be made.

Another area that might help executive and director-level staff assess and prioritize the list is to check giving records against other data available in your church management system. You should be able to answer these questions:

- Are these people or families church members?

- Do these people volunteer? If so, where and for how long?

- Have these individuals been on mission trips? If so, when was the last time they went?

- Do these people or families attend regularly?

All of these are signs of engagement. It is vital to develop a complete profile of the financial leader. If you aren't collecting this information accurately and consistently, you are hindering your ability to track key indicators of church growth and health. This information is vital to understanding a financial leader in advance of your first meeting. It's not required, but it always helps to have as much information as possible.

External Discovery Tools

There are a wide variety of discovery tools available to you should you want to use them in addition to the data you already have. Some of them are free. Some of them aren't. See "Suggested Tools to Discover Financial Leaders in Your Church" in the appendix for an expanded list.

Consider social media sites as a good place to start. Sites like Google, Facebook, Twitter, and LinkedIn often contain vital insight into individuals or families. You'd be surprised by how much information you can gather about someone online with a few simple searches.

Another place to look is on real estate sites such as Zillow and by searching public records. These are assets, and financial leaders often give from their assets, not out of their regular compensation. In fact, most financial leaders don't receive typical paychecks. Real estate and business licenses are always a good indicator of financial leaders.

There are more sophisticated tools used by many professional fundraisers who work for large nonprofit organizations that can help determine which people have the potential to make significant gifts. These tools often cost money and can be intimidating to navigate if you're not familiar with them. Once your ministry gets off the ground, these may be something to consider. For now, just know the tools exist and are available when the timing is right.

Good Intentions

We want to note that you shouldn't try to act like the FBI or CIA. You're not trying to find hidden skeletons and secrets. You simply want to know more about them, their personalities, their interests, and so on. All of this information will help you relate to financial leaders should they agree to meet with you.

The time you get with financial leaders will be limited. You want to make the most of your time together. If you are adequately prepared, you'll better guage who the person is and anticipate how they like to relate to others. It will also help getting through the awkward first meeting by finding areas where you can connect with them. Children, marriage, and hobbies are always good places to start. Sharing passions and life goals is even better.

This is not a one-time discovery process. Your church should be constantly looking for potential financial leaders. Having a team in place and a general knowledge of good discovery habits will definitely help you create a system and a process that can be managed, measured, and modified as needed.

CHAPTER SEVEN IN REVIEW

Key Ideas

1. You must create a system to identify and cultivate financial leaders. The system must be monitored and measured so you will have the data needed to evaluate the effectiveness of the ministry.

2. Giving histories and patterns will help you identify the financial leaders within your church.

3. Discuss in person with your leadership team the list of potential financial leaders. Remind them of the sensitivity of the information and the need to keep it confidential.

4. If you aren't collecting giving and participation information accurately and consistently, you are hindering your ability to track key indicators of church growth and health.

5. Your church should be constantly looking for potential financial leaders.

Key Discussion Questions

1. What is your system for identifying and cultivating financial leaders?

2. How can you monitor giving history without violating your church's privacy policy?

3. Who are three church leaders with whom you should discuss potential financial leaders?

4. What is your church's procedure for collecting giving and activity information on participants and members?

5. What are three indicators of someone who might be a financial leader?

THE MINISTRY OF GIVING IN ACTION

After watching his church's approach to ministry and assessing its effectiveness, Fred felt confident that God was leading him to step into a greater financial leadership role. Fred was moved by the way the church worked in the life of his wife and family as well as many others.

While attending a vision casting event where his senior pastor described the needs for future ministry, Fred felt led to be the top financial leader for the campaign and was. The senior pastor then began meeting with Fred relationally. During one of the meetings, the senior pastor was going to ask for a gift to a special project. Even before they met that day, though, Fred had realized he was not doing enough and felt he needed to make a gift that made him sweat. So, divinely inspired, Fred made the largest financial commitment in the church's history. Fred was happy to have the opportunity to honor God with this gift to his church.

—Eagle Brook Church (Centerville, MN)

Chapter Eight

WHAT TO EXPECT DURING YOUR FIRST MEETING

Meeting with financial leaders is a wonderful opportunity for both sides. This is a time when you will be able to share about who you are, as well as your vision, mission, and ministry plan for the church, and even the things that you are most excited about. It's also a time when you will get to know financial leaders on a personal level.

Giving always happens through relationships. Financial leaders understand what it means to be a good steward of money and resources. They want to have confidence that you can achieve the vision you have presented them. The best way to do that is to let them in and share your thoughts and ideas with them, but you'll only be able to do that interpersonally.

Before we go forward, we want to be clear that there is absolutely no substitute for in-person meetings. Technology is great, but it doesn't replace human interaction. If you are going to disciple this group, you will need to build deep relationships, which takes face-to-face interaction.

Get an Appointment

Once you have a list of financial leaders identified, you will need to set appointments to meet with them. These are busy people with full schedules. Don't just show up at their place of business or track them down in public. Respect their time by contacting them via email or phone to schedule a time to meet. (See "Sample Invitation to Meet" in the appendix.)

Expect some back-and-forth to take place before you settle on a date and time. If they prefer that you work with their administrative or personal assistant, don't take offense. The assistant keeps their schedule and will determine whether or not you make it on the calendar (or if this person is busy for the next ten years).

When initiating first meetings, assign a team member to each financial leader based on the size of the church. Here is a good guide to follow:

- If your church is *750 or less* in average weekend attendance, then the senior pastor should make the initial call.

- If your church is *between 750 and 2,000* in average weekend attendance, then a volunteer leader or dedicated staff member should make the initial call.

- If your church is *between 2,000 and 5,000* in average weekend attendance, then an executive staff member should make the initial call.

- If your church is *5,000 or more* in average weekend attendance, then an executive director or dedicated staff member should make the initial call.

These aren't necessarily hard and fast rules, but merely good starting points. You need to evaluate how you want to handle the initial contacts. Generally, the smaller the church, the more likely the senior pastor should handle the meeting, while the larger the church, the more likely an executive staff member can handle it. The more senior the financial leader, the greater the expectation will be to meet and hear from his or her peer when communicating with your church.

Decide on a Meeting Place

Depending on the time of day, suggest a public place near their office or home. It could be for breakfast, coffee, lunch, or dinner. If they ask you to come to their office, then meet them there. Very often, executives have private meeting rooms where they can meet with you. Let them decide where they would like to meet.

Be sure to confirm any appointment via email one to two days in advance. And don't be bothered if by chance it is rescheduled. They aren't trying to avoid you. Be flexible. They will appreciate that.

Wherever you meet, dress in line with your church culture. Be you. That doesn't mean show up in cut-off jeans and flip-flops. But don't put on a three-piece Armani suit if you normally wear jeans and oxford shirts during weekend church services.

Finally, plan to pay for the bill if you meet for a meal or coffee. They have given you their time. The least you can do is pick up the tab. You should know that once they trust you, they will likely be the ones who pay for lunch or coffee.

When this happens, it is a key indicator that a real relational bond is taking place.

Set the Tone

If you're at ease, they will likely be at ease. This is not the first time they've been asked by someone from a nonprofit to meet with them. You can immediately diffuse any tension by simply stating you did not schedule this meeting to ask them for money—instead, you want to thank them for giving significantly and generously to the church, and you wanted to learn more about what prompted them to do that. They'll be blown away you cared enough to say thank you. So few people and organizations take the time to do that.

This will keep the focus on them. Ask lots of questions. Listen. Take notes in a notebook if that helps you concentrate. Be sure to turn your phone on silent or vibrate. Don't check email or text messages while you meet. Give them your full attention.

Ask them about their family, their passions, how they came to the church, and mutual people you might know. Remember to balance being social with being friends. There might be a personal relationship that emerges from the time you spend together, but it won't happen during the first meeting.

Know that financial leaders are not looking for a new best friend. They give through relationships, but they give to mission, vision, and results. Keep the relationship professional and focused.

What you're listening for are clues and indicators of what's most important to them. If you listen, they will tell you what they are passionate about. These are the things they are likely to fund in a significant way. The goal is not to ask for money, but to create a common ground and give them reason to connect again. It might also be a good opportunity to connect them with the senior leader if appropriate.

Follow Up

Sending thank-you notes might seem outdated, but nothing trumps a personal, handwritten note. So few people send those anymore. It's more efficient to send an email or text. Take the extra step of sending a personal note. You will be surprised how much you stand out.

Make notes about your meeting, what you remember, and determine what your next move will be. One of the most important things the volunteer or staff leader dedicated to this role can do is connect financial leaders with the senior pastor. They want to interact with their peers and will only meet with representatives for so long.

In general, churches almost never receive gifts of $1 million or more where relationships didn't begin as a social conversation and develop over time. While there may be some exceptions, the best plan is to take the time, effort, and energy necessary to meet with financial leaders in person. When you ground conversations of money and ministry within the context of relationships, you'll be prepared when it's time to make the ask and invite financial leaders to commit in specific ways.

CHAPTER EIGHT IN REVIEW

Key Ideas

1. Giving always happens through relationships.
2. Financial leaders are unlikely to accept any substitute but your time—and eventually the time and access to the senior leader.
3. Listen for clues and indicators of what's most important to financial leaders.
4. After the meeting, send a personal, handwritten thank-you note.
5. Ground the conversation of money and ministry within the context of a relationship so you'll be prepared to ask and invite financial leaders to commit to supporting the ministry and vision.

Key Discussion Questions

1. Do you already have strong relationships with financial leaders in your church?
2. How available is the senior leader for personal conversations with financial leaders?
3. What are three or four personal interest questions you can prepare to use in every conversation?
4. What personal notes do you remember? How did it make you feel to receive them? How often do you send them to others?
5. How can you make sure financial leaders don't feel like you only want their money?

Chapter Nine

WHEN TO ASK AND WHAT FOR

You've heard it said, "If you build it, they will come." We are convinced that is only partially true. We believe: "If you build it *and ask them to come,* then they will come."

This is probably the part of the ministry of giving that can break a senior church leader into cold sweats. We've heard just about every spiritual and nonspiritual reason to avoid doing this. At the end of the day, our ability to fully fund ministry comes down to our conviction that what we are trying to accomplish is worth asking other people to support with dollars.

Ministry to financial leaders involves money because that is one way God has uniquely positioned them to serve the church. In every church, there are great counselors, great singers, great teachers, and great program directors. In addition to those vital roles, there are also great givers. The reason why they aren't giving to your church to their maximum capacity right now is likely because you haven't asked them.

Timing Is Everything

There are two contexts by which an ask will come: event-driven or project-driven. While those two things may sound similar, they are different. An event-driven ask is tied to a time-sensitive opportunity that will satisfy an immediate need. A project-driven ask is something tied to a much larger plan that might be associated with launching a new ministry, sustaining special mission work, or supporting some type of capital funds project.

Both events and projects are catalysts for you to make the ask. No matter what context in which the ask is made, you'll need a few things in advance of it.

- *Case for Support.* This is an internal document that is more an exercise for you than the financial leader. A case for support outlines what you need to fund, why you need to fund it, why you need to act on it now, and what you need to reach your funding goal. These are all important elements of any ministry plan. You'll find the clarity it brings to be empowering as you shape your messaging around whatever you're trying to accomplish.

- *Awareness of Financial Leaders.* We discussed how to identify these leaders in your church in chapter 8. But don't be too concerned if you haven't had time to accomplish this step in advance of a project-driven giving opportunity. It's always recommended to have an existing relationship with financial leaders. Sometimes that happens between special giving projects and sometimes that happens during them. Either way, you'll need to know who fits your profile for a financial leader in your church, and you'll need to know who on the executive staff has the best relationship with them.

- *Personal Conviction.* You have to be absolutely convinced that what you're about to ask someone to
fund is what God has called you to accomplish. If
you hesitate, keep practicing and working through
your case for support until it is as natural as saying
hello. If you doubt your own decision, the financial
leader will pick up on that and will be much less
likely to fund an effort—project or event—at maximum capacity.

In addition to two contexts that prompt an ask, there
are also two settings. One is in a group setting, the other
is in a personal and private setting. Both are vital and necessary for the process. When speaking to financial leaders
about very large gifts, expect that it will always happen in
a personal and private setting. Group settings can be very
healthy but are typically not the proper setting for significant gifts. While group settings can produce significant gifts,
your largest gifts will likely come from a personal ask made
in a private setting. For the purpose of this chapter, we've
chosen to focus on individual, private meetings. (You could
apply a similar approach to both settings, though.)

Core Elements of an Ask

Much of the anxiety related to an ask subsides once you
have an outline to work from. Here is a sample outline that
we suggest every leader follows:

- *Describe where your church has been.* Tell the story
of your church and highlight the times when
critical decisions were made that contributed to

significant growth and life change. This demonstrates a church's history to face obstacles, respond, and accomplish the goal.

- *Describe what God is calling your church to accomplish.* Be specific. Don't talk in philosophical terms. This is your elevator speech. You should be able to clearly articulate your goal in thirty words or less.

- *Present your plan of action.* Financial leaders rarely make any decision without calculating the different potential outcomes. Success doesn't happen by chance but is a product of opportunity and preparation. This will show financial leaders that you have carefully thought this through before meeting with them.

- *Outline your financial goals.* Everything comes at a cost. Financial leaders already know this, so tell them what they need to hear *before* they agree to fund your ministry effort.

- *Describe what God is doing now.* Share stories of life change that represent how your ministry is presently influencing the lives of real people.

- *Answer why your church is a good investment.* Articulate movements within your church such as growth patterns, fiscal disciplines, expense controls, debt management, and general fund balances. Financial leaders want to know you can make the most of the gift that they have the capacity to give.

- *Ask them for a specific gift amount.* Decide this number before the meeting. This is a combination of art and science. Make it worthy of who they are and what capacity you assess them to have. Once you've asked, pause and let them respond.

- *Challenge them to pray.* If they say yes, pray about how God will use their gift, and ask them to do the same. If the amount is significant, they may need time to think it over or even consult with their accountant or attorney. Keep the focus on what God wants to do through them. Prayer is a great way to bring the conversation back around to ministry; it's also a very comfortable way to diffuse any tension if it arises.

Making an ask is not hard if you've done your homework. If you already have an existing relationship with financial leaders, it is likely to feel even more natural. But there is no reason to dread doing it. Follow the outline above and you'll be prepared to successfully ask financial leaders to join you in expanding the Kingdom and bringing to reality the vision God has called your church to accomplish.

Rules of Thumb

We've outlined your part. Is there a way to anticipate what financial leaders will do or say? Sadly, no. We wish, but people are people. And people are full of surprises.

Consider these rules of thumb when interacting with financial leaders around an ask:

- No is rarely no. It's most likely means not now.

- The first gift is not the largest possible gift. (Even if it seems large to you.)

- They are not looking for a tax deduction.

- They don't want to be wined and dined by the church.

- They don't need a long, drawn-out presentation. Keep it short and sweet.

- You're not the first, only, or last organization who will ask them to give or to whom they will give.

- The person most likely to get the largest gifts is the most senior leader in the church.

- Financial leaders are influential in other ways too. They can influence others in their peer group and are likely respected by others within the church.

- Financial leaders want to be engaged one-on-one and not just spoken to in groups. A large gift warrants a personal, individualized touch.

Don't fret or worry. You're going to do great. Pray one last prayer before you pull in the driveway. Take a deep breath before you ask. Follow the process. And trust God to do the rest.

After the Gift Is Received

When financial leaders accept your ask and choose to invest in your ministry plan, be sure to do these things next:

- *Thank them.* Don't forget to say thank you.

- *Celebrate with them.* This is a moment of spiritual growth and movement within a person or family.

- *Ask their permission to share about the gift given—no names attached.* Let them know that you won't share with anyone without their knowledge.

(We would advise you not Tweet or update your Facebook status with this information.)

- *Alert executive staff.* If not part of the ask, make sure the senior pastor is aware of the gift pledged.

- *Define the steps to receive the gift and when the church should expect it.* They will give you instructions. Be sure to follow through with the steps provided.

- *Make sure you follow through on what they funded.* Give them updates along the way and be sure they know when what they funded has been completed.

The most important part of the outline above is to thank them. Thank them when they say yes. Send them a handwritten note a day or two after the commitment is made. The senior leader should strongly consider writing this note.

Gift Acceptance Policy

It would be wise for your church to have a gift acceptance policy in place. This will help the church decide what to do when a gift has been pledged. This is especially true with gifts-in-kind, such as personal property, real estate, businesses, and so on. You will protect yourself and the church by having one of these in place.

Your gift acceptance policy doesn't need to be complicated or even prepared by an attorney. It can be a one-page, internal document that simply follows the outline above and addresses the various details. Taking this step may seem tedious, but it is intended to protect everyone involved.

Here are some important elements of a gift acceptance policy:

- *Defines what gifts you will and will not accept.* Non-liquid assets such as real estate, personal property, or businesses can be very tricky and complicated. It's best to have the financial leader liquidate the asset and then make a cash gift to the church.

- *Defines how you will accept stock.* Go ahead and meet with your banker and financial office to determine routing numbers, bank accounts, and so on. This will save time when the gift is made.

- *Identifies who will review, approve, and follow through with the plan to receive the gift.* Appoint more than one person to sign off on the gift. Crazy things can and do happen. Someone needs to be responsible for seeing it through too.

Funding ministry happens at the intersection of need and opportunity. The clearer you can be and the more compelled you are about the direction you are headed, the greater chance you'll be able to share your vision for what God has called you to accomplish with passion. Your faith will be honored when God demonstrates an abundant provision for your ministry.

Making the ask should never be intimidating. If you will keep the focus on your defined ministry plan and the passion of the financial leader, you'll discover a moment when the two meet. It is then you'll recognize that making the ask is less about money as much as it is about facilitating a way for the financial leader to accomplish something that is important, significant, and meaningful.

CHAPTER NINE IN REVIEW

Key Ideas

1. Our ability to fully fund ministry comes down to our conviction that what we are trying to accomplish is worth asking other people to support with their dollars.

2. In every church, there are great counselors, great singers, great teachers, and great program directors. In addition to those vital roles, there are also great givers.

3. Speaking to financial leaders about very large gifts should take place in personal and private settings.

4. Financial leaders are more likely to respond positively when approached by the senior leader in the church.

5. Your church should have a simple, comprehensive gift acceptance policy in place.

Key Discussion Questions

1. What are the three most significant things your church is attempting to accomplish?

2. List significant leaders in your church—counselors, singers, teachers, program directors, and givers. What would happen if any of these people stopped supporting the ministry?

3. How comfortable are you speaking to financial leaders about making significant gifts to the ministry?

4. Why do you think financial leaders are more likely to respond positively when approached by the senior leader of the church?

5. Do you have a gift acceptance policy? When was the last time it was reviewed and updated?

The Ministry of Giving in Action

Shandon United Methodist Church is completing its third capital campaign in which I have served as Senior Minister. Each of the three campaigns has been successful at engaging and involving hundreds of church members, calling them to a higher commitment to Christian stewardship in our journey to raise needed funds for additions and renovations to our church campus. However, none of the campaigns would have been as successful without the involvement and leadership of financial leaders. In all three of these campaigns, we received the number and size of major gifts needed to meet our goal.

What I have learned is this: People who have been blessed with much want to give, and they understand that they can help a campaign in a manner most church members can't. They want to use their resources to advance the cause of Christ and the church's ministry. The approach to them is easy: just put the need before them and ask them to pray about a gift of a particular size. Major donors feel that as a result of being blessed with wealth, they have a responsibility to use what they have to bless others. I am sure that because of their wealth they are often approached about sizeable gifts to worthy causes. They expect to be asked and sometimes will be disappointed if you don't ask them. I think because of their wealth, many understand the principles to stewardship better than others. At least that is what I have observed in our three capital campaigns.

—Dr. Mike Guffee

Senior Minister, Shandon United Methodist Church (Columbia, SC)

Chapter Ten

HOW TO SUSTAIN YOUR MINISTRY TO FINANCIAL LEADERS

The next topic you will want to think through is how to sustain your effort. If you've already been implementing everything we've advised you to do up to this point, you are likely experiencing exciting things in your ministry of giving. It's only natural to wonder how to keep things moving forward.

In our experience, one of the first questions the senior pastor will ask you is, "If this works, do we have a plan for what's next?" That's usually the missing piece. Kicking up the dust is the easy part. Figuring out what to do once the dust settles can seem overwhelming, but it is crucial.

That is the final piece to the puzzle that we want to help you put together. It's not enough to just get things started. If this is really about developing and discipling people, then this is not a one-time or short-term effort. You need to be committed to this for the long haul.

Core Elements of a Sustainable Plan

To sustain something for a period of time requires focus, energy, and effort. The longer you do it, the stronger, more proficient, and more agile you'll become. Here are the parts of a sustainable plan to minister to the financial leaders in your church:

- Never stop looking for new financial leaders.

- Stay in touch with the top twenty-five givers in your church. Maintain the relationship that you worked so hard to cultivate.

- Ask for referrals from financial leaders. There is power that comes when another leader is introduced to you by a peer.

- Continue to anticipate different moments when you'll need to make an ask as a result of an event-driven or project-driven opportunity. There will be special giving opportunities throughout your ministry. Financial leaders want to participate in the big moments and the small moments.

Learn to Celebrate

Look for times to celebrate the growth as a church, in small groups, or one-on-one. We don't do this enough in the church. When we reach a significant ministry milestone, we should take a moment to celebrate what God has done. This is healthy for everyone involved.

Celebration as a church is important, but don't forget to gather the small group of people who made it possible to achieve that ministry goal and bring the vision to life. Honor the role that they played.

This will be an excellent opportunity to let them see the outcomes of their work. You can only do so many dinners, focus groups, and the like. Eventually, these events become stale and formulaic. You asked for partnership because of a relationship, so celebration in a relational context makes sense. Be sure to stay consistent with the culture of your church. Don't try to be something or someone that you're not.

At these celebration events, be sure the senior leader is there. We can't say enough about how important financial leaders' interaction with the senior leader is. This is one of the unique roles that only the senior leader can fill. During this time, encourage the group to share what their participation and contribution to the event or project has meant to them. We would suggest asking one or two to share in advance. This will help get the group moving forward.

Next Steps

If you're not going into a capital funds project, then:

- Start forming small groups of financial leaders. Two couples work best. Always include the spouses.

- Give them regular, personal updates when ministry goals and progress have been made.

- Be sure to discern the makeup of the couples and try to match them with complementary personalities.

- Follow up with the entire group individually about twice a year. Phone and email are fine. One annual, in-person meeting is preferred.

- Consider hosting a retreat where the senior pastor can share more about the vision for the church and invite the group of financial leaders to share their interests, passions, and vision. (See "Sample Agenda for a Financial Leaders Retreat" in the appendix.)

- Coordinate trips for financial leaders to observe the difference their gifts are making. These can be very formative trips for everyone involved.

- Invite a small group of financial leaders to go with you to visit another church to see something you might be interested in doing in your church. Learn from them. Let the financial leaders into the early phases of the planning process. They are more likely to feel like they own it.

- Look for ways to keep financial leaders engaged, and you'll be ready when it's time to invite them to make another financial gift to accomplish the mission and vision of your church.

If you are going into a capital funds project, then start with focus groups:

- Gather a group of twenty-five or so couples (could be larger or smaller depending on the size of your church) for a special meeting.

- Present your case for support to this group. Invite their feedback, participation, and leadership in making a commitment. This is a great way to test-run your presentation and will be the last time you are able to refine your case for support before you present it to the church.

- Know that when you use their feedback, it becomes theirs. There is a transfer of ownership because they had a hand in it.

- Remember to keep things at the big-picture level. Don't go too far into the details or you will lose people. You're likely six to nine months out from launching the campaign. Many small details will still need to be worked out.

As the campaign approaches:

- Conduct at least six to ten one-on-one meetings to get buy-in and support. These are the people you will need to make significant gifts during the campaign. Inviting them in early allows them to do what they do best—troubleshoot and ensure the church's success. Tell them they are the first ones to hear about the details and you want their feedback and insight. They will be glad to help.

- Determine your gift plan. Estimate the different size gifts your financial leaders are likely to make. Refer back to chapter 9 to refresh your memory on what the ask will look like.

- Make sure you conduct these meetings three to four weeks in advance of the first commitment gathering for the campaign.

- The senior pastor should be involved with every one-on-one. These meetings are critical for your success during the initial commitment phase of a campaign.

The one-on-ones could take place in advance of any large gathering of financial leaders. Their feedback will influence your message that night. The senior and executive pastors might even split up the presentation. Let the executive pastor talk about why, what, and why now. Then the senior pastor will be positioned for the most emotional part of the evening— the vision plan and commitment time.

Keep Moving Forward

Sustaining any effort takes a lot of work. But it's possible. And the church leaders will have to invest the time, staff, and resources to create a sustainable ministry of giving that will produce results beyond any single event or project.

The most important thing you can do is stay in motion. You will learn in the midst of the doing. If you wait until you have it all figured out, you'll never get started.

God is on your side, as well as financial leaders in your church who want to play an active role in meeting the needs of people in your community and around the world. They believe in God's ability to change lives as much as you do, and they recognize they have unique resources to do that. Ensuring a strong, healthy, and long relationship with the financial leaders in your church will also ensure that the resources God has blessed them with flow to the things God is most passionate about—total life transformation.

CHAPTER TEN IN REVIEW

Key Ideas

1. Every capital initiative should be a discipleship process. Without discipleship, nothing long-term will happen.

2. You must maintain constant communication with the top twenty-five givers in your church.

3. Churches should routinely celebrate God's work.

4. Financial leaders must be updated on the progress of the ministry.

5. God is not the only one on your side. There are financial leaders in your church who want to play an active role in meeting the needs of people in your community and around the world.

Key Discussion Questions

1. Is your emphasis on giving short-term or part of an ongoing discipleship strategy?

2. What are three things you can do to maintain constant communication with the top twenty-five givers in your church?

3. How does your church celebrate God's activity?

4. Why is it important to keep financial leaders updated on the progress of the ministry?

5. God brought financial leaders to your church to support the ministry. What does this fact say about God's plans for your church?

CONCLUSION

The most effective step church leaders can take to significantly expand their church's ministry capacity is to establish a special giving ministry focused on discovering and developing their financial leaders. We've discussed the why, what, and how involved in doing so. The next step is really up to you.

To encourage you, I (Kimberly) want to share some of the things we have experienced at Eagle Brook Church since implementing an intentional ministry of giving to financial leaders in our church. We tracked the top one hundred givers in our church and noticed these changes:

- From 2009 to 2010 total giving increased 23 percent
- From 2010 to 2011 total giving increased 55 percent
- From 2011 to 2012 total giving increased 61 percent

Our top 100 represent 33 percent of Eagle Brook's total giving for the calendar year 2012. I also think it is worth mentioning that everyone should not expect these same results. Our experience at Eagle Brook is specific to our church and the amazing things God is doing in our ministry. However, I want you to be encouraged by the potential outcomes that could take place in your church. Of course, these numbers don't show the value of the spiritual growth that has taken place within the lives of this group as well as the people who have benefited from the ministries this group had a significant role in funding.

Next Steps

This book was never meant to be exhaustive. We like to think of it as an invitation to a great adventure. Will you act on the opportunity that is before you?

We hope this field guide will help you get started. Be sure to keep a copy on your desk or bookshelf for future reference. It would also be a good tool to use with other staff leaders who might join you in this effort. Doing so will ensure a common language and practice is shared among a small group of people.

If there is any interest at all in moving forward with a giving ministry in your church, we encourage you to take these immediate next steps:

- *Pray about it.* Be sure this is the direction God is leading you right now. Timing is everything. And no amount of human ingenuity or tenacity will be able to overcome the lack of God's blessing. Don't fear being first, but don't rush to be first either. Also, establishing a ministry of giving is not a "quick fix" to a difficult financial situation; it's a commitment to a long-term engagement with a key segment of your congregation whom God intends to use to fund the ministry of the church.

- *Talk with your executive or senior-level team.* Make sure they understand what you're thinking and what you hope to accomplish. If you move forward, you'll need them to be completely on board with you. This becomes even more important as the front-line ministry staff become aware of your effort. Launching a ministry of giving should be a "we" decision, not a "me" decision.

- *Consult with at least one financial leader in your church.* Get feedback and input. You're going to need their support, and you'll need one or two to be on your initial team as we discussed in chapter 6. They will be your insiders who will help you navigate new waters and maximize your opportunity in the early days of this ministry.

- *Step out in faith.* You will need to trust the process. Keep your focus on relationships and spiritual development. Pray that God will protect your heart in the process. Then act with boldness and confidence just as you've done a number of times before in other areas of your ministry.

God's Vision Fully Funded

Launching a giving ministry isn't about money. It's about raising people to fulfill the mission and vision God has placed on your heart. To see God's vision fully funded isn't about celebrating a financial goal. What we celebrate is the ministry that can take place now that the resources and leadership are available to make it possible.

Life change is the currency used within the Kingdom of God. The truth is that God has already given your church all the people, money, and talent you need to take the next step toward your God-inspired vision. The missing piece is your willingness to do the work to make sure everyone is fully engaged in Kingdom things and experiencing spiritual growth as a result of it.

We believe God wants to do something amazing in your church. It will require you to do things that might feel uncomfortable or familiar. But we've seen God take the courage of leaders willing to take this step of faith and use it to advance the ministry of a church in exponential ways. We believe that can happen for you and your church too.

ABOUT THE AUTHORS

Joel Mikell is president of RSI. With more than twenty-five years of local church ministry experience, he brings a passion for helping churches cast their vision to reach people for Christ, as only a pastor can. He has helped church leaders raise more than $500 million for Kingdom projects and has had the privilege of working with some of the most well-known churches and church leaders across the country. Joel can be reached at joel.mikell@rsistewardship.com, Twitter (@joelmikell), or Facebook (www.facebook.com/joel.mikell).

Bill McMillan served for more than twenty years as both a pastor and a pastoral counselor before joining RSI. He currently serves as executive vice president. Bill has led thriving stewardship campaigns in churches of many sizes and denominations, raising millions of dollars for local ministry. He is an excellent communicator and project manager, whose consulting hallmarks lie in communications strategy and major gift development. Bill can be reached at bill.mcmillan@rsistewardship.com, Twitter (@billmcmillanrsi), or Facebook (www.facebook.com/bill.mcmillan.52).

Kimberly Stewart is the executive director of development for Eagle Brook Church in the Twin Cities, responsible for overseeing the financial leader development strategy across its five campuses. Prior to joining Eagle Brook four years ago, Kimberly had a successful career as a corporate sales executive developing and expanding the relationship between her clients and the IT research advisory firm that employed her. Her transition from the corporate sector to her role in ministry came naturally and has allowed her to fully embrace her passion for generosity and involvement in her church. Kimberly can be reached at kimberly.stewart@eaglebrookchurch.com.

APPENDIX

The following are examples and samples that may work depending upon your church culture.

Sample Job Description for Executive Director

Sample Invitation to Meet

Sample Thank-You Letter

Sample Agenda for a Financial Leaders Retreat

10 Things Financial Leaders Will Do *Before* They Will Fund Ministry

Suggested Tools to Discover Financial Leaders in Your Church

Scripture Directed to Financial Leaders

Suggested Reading

SAMPLE JOB DESCRIPTION FOR EXECUTIVE DIRECTOR

Job Title: Executive Director of Development

Classification: Full Time/Exempt

Department: Development

Reports to: Executive Pastor

Purpose: The purpose of the executive director of development is to create and manage a comprehensive development program to increase annual revenue for ministries.

Education, Skills, Abilities, Spiritual Gifts:

- Vital and growing relationship with Jesus Christ
- BA/BS degree
- High-level experience and proven skills in working within a large organization
- Prior development experience a plus
- Effective communication skills: interpersonal, written, and verbal
- Strong relational and team-building skills
- Problem-solving skills
- Demonstrated leadership ability, especially one-on-one
- Spiritual gifts: leadership, administration, giving

Competencies and Expectations:

- Embrace and embody the mission
- Be reliable, take initiative, and be self-motivated
- Embrace and adapt to growth, change, innovation, and creativity
- Use appropriate judgment in the areas of discretion, sensitivity, and confidentiality
- Have a cooperative, healthy, and motivating relationship with supervisors and coworkers

Essential Functions:

- Develop and implement strategies to grow income streams, including funds raised through individual and institutional gifts, special events, etc.
- Develop and implement an annual development operational plan and budget
- Supervise and coordinate events as needed
- Lay the groundwork and implement an effective planned giving program
- Manage a portfolio of major giver prospects to cultivate, solicit, and steward
- Play a significant role in developing and implementing campaigns, as needed

SAMPLE INVITATION TO MEET

Hello, Bob and Sue,

My name is [name], and I am the executive director of development at [church]. I am in the process of getting to know some of our attendees, and I would love to set up a time to get to know you and thank you for your amazing support of our mission.

Would you be available to meet sometime during the week of April 19 or the week of April 26 for coffee? I realize that life is busy, so if those weeks don't work for you, please let me know and I will arrange my schedule to accommodate your suggested time.

I look forward to hearing from you, and thank you again for all you do!

Sincerely,

SAMPLE THANK-YOU LETTER

Hello, Bob and Sue,

Thank you so much for taking the time out of your schedule to meet with me this week. It was a pleasure getting to know you both and hearing your incredible story. I will be sending you the information we discussed, and I'm available at any time to answer any additional questions you may have regarding the ministry.

We are truly blessed to have you as part of the [church] family and can't thank you enough for deciding to make a difference and invest in what God is doing in our church. We couldn't do what we do without you!

I look forward to seeing you at church.

Blessings,

SAMPLE AGENDA FOR A FINANCIAL LEADERS RETREAT

Schedule Overview

Friday

3 p.m.—Check-in begins at Swan Lake (Name Tags/ Agenda/Notes of encouragement waiting for them in rooms)

7 to 8 p.m.—Dessert (Ballroom Salons II & III)

8 to 9:30 p.m.—Session 1 (Ballroom Salon I)

9:30 p.m.—Open Evening

Saturday

7:30 to 8:30 a.m.—Breakfast Buffet (Ballroom Salons II & III)

9 to 10 a.m.—Session 2 (Ballroom I)

10 a.m. to Noon—Free Time

Noon—Hotel Check-out Time

Noon to 1 p.m.—Luncheon Buffet (Ballroom Salons II & III)

1 to 2 p.m.—Session 3 (Ballroom Salon I)

2 p.m.—End of Retreat

Schedule Details

Session 1 (Friday, 8 to 9:30 p.m.)—Connect with God

8 p.m.—Welcome & Introduction

- Share what this weekend IS (chance to connect with each other, relax, ask questions, learn).

- Tell them what this weekend is NOT (a fundraiser; relax, there will not be an "ask").

- Let them know who is in the room (you are not surrounded by rich people; some have asked, "How did I get invited?"—it's because you are generous, and a whole bunch of people in the church are generous, people just like you; there are other generous people who were invited who could not come so don't assume these are the only generous people).

- Why do this retreat? (If you were in the band, we'd gather you together and find a way to connect; if you worked in the nursery, we'd gather you and say thanks and help you get to know each other; why would we not also do that if you are exercising your gift of generosity?)

9 p.m.—Closing Thoughts

- This is time for you to share whatever God is teaching you, what you are learning, thinking, etc.

9:25 p.m.—Announcements

- Hand out Q&A card for tomorrow.

- The Bible says that when you give your money to a certain place, your heart goes with your money.

- That means you are more invested, you have greater ownership where you give your money, you have different questions than people who are not as invested, and we want to know your questions. We will take time to answer them tomorrow morning, but we need to know what they are. Ask anything. No limits! We will get to as many of them as we can in the morning.

9:28 p.m.—Closing prayer

Session 2 (Saturday, 9 to 10 a.m.)— Inside Information / Ask Anything / Q&A

- Have handout of Inside Information (reports) on the tables.

- Answer anything they ask (be sure they have submitted questions ahead of time).

Session 3 (Saturday, 1 to 2 p.m.)— Hear from Each Other

- Ask financial leaders to tell God stories. (You are the church—you see God working in places we never will—unless you tell us! Where have you seen God at work through the ministry and people of the church in recent days?)

- Challenge them, not hesitating to ask them to do everything they can do. (Keep doing what you do. Keep serving as God has wired you. Keep sharing your story of faith. Keep giving strongly, consistently, and sacrificially. This vision from God is bigger than each of us. None of us can do it by ourselves. But all of us can do it together.)

- Closing—pray a blessing over everyone as they leave.

10 THINGS FINANCIAL LEADERS WILL DO *BEFORE* THEY FUND MINISTRY

1. Evaluate your preparedness for the meeting and the project.

2. Ask lots of questions.

3. Look for potential return on investment (e.g., impact, life transformation).

4. Ask for information and regular updates.

5. Meet with senior leadership.

6. Take an appropriate amount of time and conversation to make a serious decision.

7. Read through your case (or business plan) for support.

8. Get to know you.

9. Look for church leaders to follow through with commitments made.

10. Expect discretion and confidentiality.

SUGGESTED TOOLS TO DISCOVER FINANCIAL LEADERS IN YOUR CHURCH

There are several ways to get lists of potential financial leaders. This can be done by running weekly reports. Are you seeing a trend with a giver or a significant gift? By running monthly and yearly reports, you can determine your top financial leaders. Is there a new person on the list who you did not see on your other reports?

You should also have a great relationship with your finance team. They can let you know when there are significant gifts through stocks or foundations. Ideally, you will have a system that will allow you to see all stock and foundation gifts in a monthly time frame. Has someone given several small gifts of stock over a month or sixth-month period that adds up to a more significant amount?

Your staff can also be a great asset by letting you know if there is someone you should follow up with.

Google

You will be very surprised at what you can find by doing a basic name search. The search should be done by individual name (husband and wife), as well as by household name.

Individual name searches can often find:

- Work information: Do they own their own business?

- Salary or stocks given as part of compensation
- College
- Hobbies
- Political donations
- Work bios

Household searches often turn up:

- Philanthropic giving
- Joint business information
- Marriage and divorce dates
- Children

As with all Google searches, you must keep in mind the information that can lead to additional information. If you see a brief mention of an old business in a newspaper article, you will want to search for that business name. Was that person the owner, was the business sold, how much did it sell for? As long a business is public, you can often find this information. If it's a private company you can often find this information in news articles or in blogs.

Don't give up on your search too quickly. The best information is often found several pages into a search of an obscure article that briefly mentions their name. Be patient and tenacious, and you will find the information.

Facebook

Oftentimes we can find out information regarding a financial leader by finding them on Facebook. If the name is common, try matching the financial leader by looking for mutual friends, church members, or church staff. You can also match by looking for the spouses name in the "married to" field, or by searching for the spouse in their friends. As long as the accounts are fairly public, you can learn a lot by looking at the profile. People will share their workplace, what college they attended, spouse, younger children at home or older children with families of their own, etc. You can also determine hobbies through photos. Consider grabbing a shot of the Facebook profile picture for the profile record that you are creating. And through the associations on Facebook, you can see other interests related to politics, hobbies, or work.

LinkedIn

LinkedIn is a great site to discover what a person does for a living. When there are several people with the same name on the site, make sure that you narrow your search by your state (or states if you are close to a state border). You will also want to search by full legal name (e.g., Jonathon Smith) and by nickname (e.g., John Smith). The search will sometimes take into account the nickname, but not always.

Make sure to then run a Google search on the business name if the person is listed as any of the following:

- Owner
- CEO
- CFO
- President

There are times that there may be multiple listing under their current job. When this happens, it often means that they own or are partners in these organizations. Research all of them to see what you can find regarding your financial leader.

What if you aren't sure if the financial leader is a match?

You can often rely on the degree of separation that appears in the upper right hand corner of their profile. If there are multiple people with the same name, the degree of separation can help you decide who to look at first to determine if they are the financial leader you are looking for. Review the "how are you connected" section. If they are connected with someone from your church, you should further research the person by using their company information—work bios can provide a lot of information!

Manta

Manta.com is a great site to search if you think your financial leader may be a business owner or if you know a company name but aren't sure if the giver is a principal or owner of the company. Manta will give you a description of what the company does, how many employees it has, and its annual revenue. This is a great way to determine if a business is large or small, and if the owner possibly has the capacity to make a gift.

Zillow

For every possible financial leader, you should search Zillow. com to gain information on his or her home. You can use this information to determine if they are upside down on their house or if they purchased the home when the market was low. These are all great indicators of whether the giver could make an asset gift.

Wealth Search Engines

There are numerous wealth search engines that you can use to find out more in-depth public information about your attendees. A few great ones to look into are Research Point and

Wealth Engine. These programs pull biographical, asset, and affiliation data that you can use for your one-on-one meetings. They can also let you know of the potential gift someone is able to make based on assets and can give you more information about potential businesses or organizations. You will need to verify and confirm all of the information that the reports pull, especially if your giver has a common name.

SELECT SCRIPTURES DIRECTED TO FINANCIAL LEADERS

"Command those who are rich in this present world not to be arrogant nor put their hope in wealth, which is so uncertain, but to put their hope in God, who richly provides us with everything for our enjoyment. Command them to do good, to be rich in good deeds, and to be generous and willing to share. In this way, they will lay up treasures for themselves as a firm foundation for the coming age, so that they may take hold of the life that is truly life." (1 Timothy 6:17–19)

"A generous man will prosper; he who refreshes others will himself be refreshed." (Proverbs 11:25)

"A generous man will himself be blessed, for he shares his food with the poor." (Proverbs 22:9)

"From everyone who has been given much, much will be demanded; and from the one who has been entrusted with much, much more will be asked." (Luke 12:48b)

"Remember the Lord your God, for it is He who gives you the ability to produce wealth." (Deuteronomy 8:18a)

"The earth is the Lord's and everything in it!" (Psalm 24:1a)

"The silver is mine and the gold is mine, declares the Lord Almighty." (Haggai 2:8)

"You are not your own; you were bought with a price." (1 Corinthians 6:19b–20a)

"Remember this: Whoever sows sparingly will also reap sparingly, and whoever sows generously will also reap generously." (2 Corinthians 9:6)

SUGGESTED READING

Books Specific to Church Ministry

- *Church Giving Matters: More Money Really Does Mean More Ministry* (2nd Ed.) by Joel Mikell and Ben Stroup

- *Uncharitable* by Dan Pallotta

- *Passing the Plate* by Christian Smith, Michael Emerson, and Patricia Snell

- *Growing Givers' Hearts* by Thomas H. Jeavons and Rebekah Basinger

- *In Pursuit of the Almighty's Dollar* by James Hudnut-Beumler

- *How to Increase Giving in Your Church* by George Barna

- *A Theology of Stewardship* by Joel Mikell

Books for General Nonprofits

- *Nonprofit Essentials: Major Gifts* by Julie Walker

- *Developing Major Gifts* by Laura Fredricks

- *The Artful Journey Cultivating and Soliciting the Major Gift* by William T. Sturtevant

- *Conducting a Successful Major Gifts and Planned Giving Program* by Kent Dove

- *Major Donors: Finding Big Gifts in Your Database and Online* by Ted Hart, James M. Greenfield, Pamela M. Gignac, and Christopher Carnie

- *Fundraising Principles and Practice* by Adrian Sargeant and Jen Shang

BOOKS AND OTHER RESOURCES
AVAILABLE FROM RSI

www.RSIStewardship.com

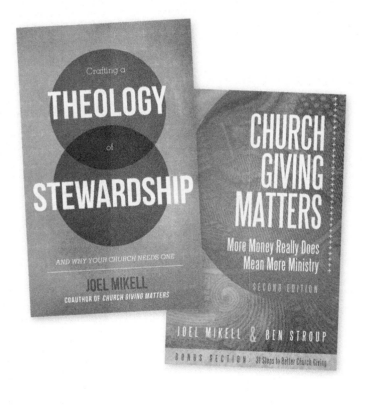

Made in the USA
Coppell, TX
04 May 2022

77405947R00080